Profitable Poultry Farming

Poultry farming business from beginner's perspective

Dr. Leonard Charles

Profitable Poultry Farming

Poultry farming business from beginner's perspective

Empower Yourself through Poultry Farming Agribusiness

Hi, would you like to start a profitable poultry hen farming business in your location? Do you need help in setting up and run your poultry farming business, professionally so that you won't make mistakes that could lead to loss of your investment? Then this is your golden book.

One good thing about this book (which most others out there don't have) is that, it contains marketing and business parts of poultry farming. My goal is to make you a poultry entrepreneur. So in this book, you'll not just learn how to raise hens; you'll also learn how to be an entrepreneur.

I have met so many farmers including my parents, making mistakes in poultry farming business and losing their money.

How can people work hard (for 5-10 years) to save money then put the money into a business, only to make mistakes and lose it all? That's painful and I don't want it to happen to you.

That's the reason why I wrote this book to help you with my years of experience in the global business and poultry farming world.

You may not know anything about business or poultry farming but this book will enlighten you if you go alone into this hen rearing business you may fail, but if you go with my book you could use my knowledge and experiences and succeed.

About The Writer

Dear friend, brother, sister, father or mother, this is

Dr. Leonard Charles, a father five. A Scholar, Researcher, businessman and I love entrepreneurship so **much**.

After spending almost all my adult life in the business world, I can't stop being ANGRY that I live in a generation where school brainwashes everyone about job.

Apart from being a businessman, I have a mission in my life to train one million personnel on how to be successful business owners. I think it is wise of us as adults, at this terrible time, to continue teaching our children and youths how to be employees.

My goal is to liberate my world from poverty. But I alone cannot do it. I need you to be part of this vision.

I started my first business before I was 18. If You Want to Learn My Secrets then read this book and more of my business training books and I will see you at the top.

A tree they said cannot make a forest and no man is an island, every man has become a necessary chain in the society of collective efforts and mutual interdependence. Please note that I do not claim to know it all and not making claim at being the number one expert on poultry farming.

However, it should be noted that with this will expose to you all I have acquired through many years of in-depth research and findings on local available raw material which have been carefully tested and documented to make you successful in poultry business, and help you achieve your goal, dreams, vision and aid your chosen field of career in livestock farming. You now become a blessing to your generation. It is all about becoming the best in business. It is about maximizing your innate abilities and corresponding transformation into wealth. About exceeding all your poultry challenges, being totally fulfilled, knowing that you did all you could and more to achieve your goal and fly higher like eagle.

Get ready to be empowered to become all you were created and crafted for. Here's to your all round success in poultry business. Work harder and think smarter. A scholar, Jim Rohr said "you might not be able to change your destination overnight but you can change your direction overnight" Start well by making this book your daily companion before and after going into the poultry business

Introduction

Poultry Farming For Beginners

As you are reading this book today, I will be taking you by the hand and showing you how to start and make money from **poultry farming business globally** and especially African countries. No. This is not going to be like other poultry business hypes and mere theories you have read before on the internet.

I have received many calls and WhatsApp messages in the past months from different Agripreneurs and my online students all over the world. Some of these people (unfortunately) called me after they have already made some serious mistakes and there were nothing or little I could do to help them anymore.

If you're reading this book about poultry farming before you start (or before you make any serious mistake), I congratulate you. Make sure you give all of your attention as I will share with you many things about poultry business you may not find elsewhere. If you forfeit your one week hang out with friends and read this book properly, you have made a good bargain.

Please forgive me as I will *assume* that you do not know anything about poultry farming business before now, so I will start from the elementary.

Now let`s get started.

Poultry farming has already proven to be a lucrative business, that you may be willing to start a farm for your new source of income. In broad, poultry farming means raising various types of domestic birds commercially for the purpose of meat, eggs and feather production. But here we are describing poultry farming for beginners guide about chickens. Chicken's products are among the major source of animal protein, aside from beef, pork and fish. And chickens are already an integral part of human life that has no cultural or tribal discrimination.

Small scale poultry production fulfills the animal nutrition demand for a family. But large scale or commercial basis poultry farming offer an opportunity for the people to earn big amount of money. That's why there are many poultry farms out there. Poultry farming is a suitable business for the people who are passionate about livestock farming, keeping birds and who are comfortable with farm life.

Poultry farming is a highly profitable business if you can run it properly under acceptable methods and conditions conducive for the birds. Actually each type of farming business follows specific operational principles for making good profit. And when such principles are ignored by the farm management system, it results in serious loses and heartbreak.

So before starting, it is wise to learn more about the business. Take some time and try to understand why most of the poultry farmers make good profits and some of them fail. Some of the farmers, especially beginners have been forced out of the business when they could not operate it properly and thus lose money. Successful poultry farming business is involved with lot of works and it's easy at the same time. But it's not a lazy man's business. You have to do everything timely and perfectly according to a plan. However, here in this book am trying to discuss details about poultry farming from beginner's perspective.

Table of Content

Contents

Chapter 1

Planning Your Poultry Hens Business

In this chapter, I will be sharing with you most important things you want to know about **poultry farming business in Nigeria.**

Poultry farming is majorly practiced in Nigeria in small scale, mostly for domestic consumption. However, this book will go beyond that. We will focus on how you can make money by raising chicken. The most common poultry bird in Nigeria is chicken.

Please forgive me as I will *assume* that you do not know anything about poultry business before now, so I will start from the elementary stage.

Let`s start.

INTRODUCTION

The dependence of man on protein from livestock and the desire of the livestock farmers to see his animals express their full genetic potential necessitate a proper management of such animals.

"Poultry farming is a very profitable business" A statement you hear anytime you make inquires about poultry business. What makes it very profitable is what this manual or guide intends to give you. Like any other investment, the poultry farming needs to be studied before being undertaken. I therefore advice you to follow all that is mentioned in this professional guide. You will save yourself the trouble of spending unnecessarily. This guide has tried to put down the key points to be observed regarding poultry housing, feeding, vaccination and general information necessary for a profitable business

What is poultry farming?

Wikipedia defines poultry farming as rearing of domesticated birds such as chickens, turkeys, ducks, and geese, for the purpose of farming meat or eggs for food. Poultry farms are farms where birds (of different nature) are raised, either for personal consumption or for commercial purposes.

Now I want to make two assumptions.

First, you're likely to be reading this book with the intention to go into poultry farming as a business.

Second, you're likely to have interest much more in chicken than other birds, since Mr. and Miss Chicken happen to be the most populous poultry birds. On these two assumptions will this book base.

Poultry products are in high demand. Poultry Business in Nigeria is a big business that gives enough meat and eggs for daily consumption of people. Eggs and chicken meat gives the necessary protein that the body needs. There is a popular slogan from the poultry farmers association that goes thus "Eat an egg a day it is good for your daily growth". To be a poultry farmer means you can be a boss of your own.

Do you know there are four common categories of birds you can start a poultry with namely; Layers, Broilers, Cockerels and Turkey?

Are you looking for a business to invest in? Are you interested in poultry farming business? Then I advise you should read on as I will be sharing with you strategic information on how to start a poultry farming business from scratch and grow it successfully.

Poultry farming is a business you would enjoy doing; it is an interesting business, very lucrative, though it is capital intensive. The poultry industry is a broad one. There are many sub-sectors in the poultry business which you can tap into. Below are arms in the poultry business:

POULTRY MANAGEMENT

Poultry management entails the provision of an enabling environment or conditions such as adequate housing, care, feeding, hygiene, etc in all phases of growth or production so that the animals can perform well. This will require an understanding of the management practices of different poultry breeds and species.

POULTRY PRODUCTION

The term poultry used in agriculture generally refers to all domesticated birds kept for eggs or meat production. These include chickens (domestic fouls) turkeys, ducks and geese. The most common of these in Nigeria are the domestic fowls. Sometimes, the term poultry is considered synonymous with chickens. Turkeys are raised in Nigeria on government experimental farms and sometimes by private farmers. The principles of management, outlined for chickens in this guide can be generally applied to other domestic birds

IMPORTANCE OF POULTRY

❖ Poultry meat and eggs are excellent forms of human food.

❖ Rearing of birds serves as a hobby for some people.

❖ The feathers are used for making feather meals with high protein content.

❖ Eggs are used for producing various vaccines.

❖ Poultry manure (Guano) is a source of plant food in the soil.

❖ Employment is provided by the poultry industry through rearing, processing, transportation, marketing etc. of birds and bird's products.

❖ Poultry enterprises are means of income to poultry farmers.

❖ Birds are high economic converters of feed. A day old broiler chick can attain a market weight of 2.5kg to 3.5kg at eight weeks. Layers may be produced within twenty weeks

❖ A poultry enterprise requires a low capital investment to establish.

❖ Birds are used for scientific experiments because they mature within a relatively short period.

What aspect of poultry farming will you love to start?

Broilers breeding

This is for meat production. You'll grow your broilers and sell them out to the consumers. Broilers grow so fast. Within 42 - 45 days, most broilers are grown and ready to be sold

Layers breeding

Here you are breeding your layer chickens with the major aim of having them laying eggs, though you'll eventually sell them off after they are becoming weak and are no longer laying eggs as expected (this is usually after 68-70 weeks, about 1 year and 4 months) and they are at this stage called spent layers.

Noiler Hens

Noiler chickens can be reared both for eggs and meat. These chickens needed to be fed for six or more months before they will start laying eggs, though they don't lay as much eggs as layers. Some of them that are reared for meat as well take much longer time to mature than broilers.

Poultry feed production.

People in this branch of poultry farming are producing poultry`s food and selling them to the poultry farmers

Hatchery

Here you have people who hatch chicken and other birds. This aspect of poultry business is very important (though not common) because the health of a bird is determined by the effectiveness of the hatchery process.

Poultry equipment manufacturing

You guess it. These guys manufacture various types equipment needed on the poultry farming.

Poultry Consultant

You will need experience in aforementioned niches before you can succeed as a consultant.

Yes, a giant company may be doing all of the above together, but if you`re just starting out, you definitely cannot, because of these two or three reasons;

☐   Taking all of the above together will require so much capital, but not just that.

☐ Starting all the above together will not work because, poultry, like any other business has a learning curve. For example, when you see a company doing all the above together, their story may look something like: Starting with layers for some months, going in to broilers, expanding to poultry feed production, later hatchery and since they might have spent many years by now, they can now venture into poultry consultancy. I`m sure you got that. Start somewhere. Learn and grow.

Crisis management

Did you hear someone said poultry business is very risky? That's not true. Every business is risky, not just poultry. Starting all the above together (even if you have enough capital) is not advisable because you are putting too many food in your mouth at a time.

Poultry Farming is probably one of the most lucrative farming businesses you can do in Nigeria especially when it is setup and managed properly. It is also the most convenient for all and sundry. The business and the civil class can comfortably key into it. You can put a cage at your back yard and rear it. The farmers we currently have, are not producing enough poultry and will not be enough even in the next ten years! This aspect of livestock farming presents one of the finest opportunities for entrepreneurs to make good money within the shortest period of time possible. This is made possible due to the quick maturity of chickens.

With over 200 Million consumers in the country who buys and eats poultry products on daily basis, the market is always here waiting to be tapped. The demand for eggs is so high that people go about everyday looking for where to buy eggs for supply.

So, how exactly can anyone who wishes to start poultry farming in Nigeria be able to go about it and come out very profitable? This book will cover a lot of ground, and it is written based on personal experience and continually updated to make sure the information here is as accurate as possible at all time.

This chapter will take more critical look at the business and how entrepreneurs who are interested in this business in any part of the world could start easily without wasting much time and resources.

Anyone can engage in poultry business, it doesn't matter your educational or financial background, you can start at any level and grow as big as you want with time. The most important thing is that you are interested in starting somewhere.

This book will focus on how to start small and grow big which I think will interest anyone with limited financial capacity who wants to start small without involving many risks.

One of the factors that make poultry business ideal business is because chickens grow very fast. Unlike goats that take 2 to 3 years to mature, a chicken can be ready for the market within 28 weeks from birth. That is why it is considered ideal business for loan takers who may actually invest the loan and within 30 to 40 weeks, they may start paying back through the money realized from sells.

PROFIT POTENTIAL IN POULTRY BUSINESS

1. Chickens do reproduce fast and in large numbers

Average healthy Layer lays egg almost every day or at least 4 times in a week. Some Breeds can lay as much as 325 eggs in a year and take 21 days to hatch. This means that technically a Layer is capable of producing another chicken twice in three days. So, if you have 500 healthy layers of good breeds (such as California white) they are capable of reproducing a whooping **12,000** chicks within 40 days!

2. Chicken grows very fast

Within 21 days, the egg is hatched and within 28 weeks, they are ready for the market. That means a farmer may start making his money in just 34 weeks after successfully setting up his farm and whatever returns he make could be doubled in a year based on this calculation.

3. Chicken sells at a very good price

A fully grown healthy chicken sells between ₦1600 **to ₦ 2, 500**. Therefore, if you produce 1,000 chickens in your farm, you will be making **₦1, 600,000 to ₦2, 500,000** by the time they are completely sold.

4. Egg market is Large too

Apart from the chicken, the egg is money of its own. A tray of eggs sells for ₦1300 to ₦1550 for smaller eggs and N1700 to ₦1800 for bigger ones. Each tray contains 30 eggs. Therefore, if you have

500 layers that produce 5 eggs in a week each at minimum therefore in a month you will have collected 10,000 eggs and decides to sell all, you will be making ₦**333, 000** monthly just from eggs selling.

As you can see, the profit in poultry farming in Nigeria is mouth watering and the turn over time is fantastic as well, but the big question now is how to start.

What Your Poultry Business Plan Should Look Like

Draw out your effective business plan. Poultry business plan is like a road map leading you to where you are going in your business. It will help you know where you are at any point in time. Hence your business plan should include:

1. Type of Bird you want to concentrate on:

Here you choose Chickens (*Layers, Indigenous breed* or *Broilers).* I choose chicken because that's what this book focuses on. There are other types of birds that are good for livestock business too, such as **Goose**, **Duck**, **Turkey**, etc

2. Write down your area of interest

You can't just be in all aspect of poultry farming in Nigeria. You have to choose your area of interest where you would like to concentrate your business. This will ensure high level of focus and professionalism. If you can do more than one, no problem below are some of the major Niches in Poultry Farming in Nigeria or elsewhere in the world.

☐   *Layers Breeding* which is egg production layers

☐   *Broilers breeding* which referrers to the chicken meat production by *Broilers*

☐   *Hatchery* which has to do with breeding chicken for the purpose of *Hatching new chicks*

☐   *Poultry feed* which is producing feeds for other poultry farmers

You may choose to Breed Layers and Broilers at a time or one of them. Hatchery is better done independently just like feed production. So, you choose your area of focus.

3. Sort out Location

This has a direct effect to your startup cost. A location in a very remote rural area will cost far less than the one close to the urban area. Remote rural area with good road is the ideal location as you will be free from regulatory agencies and drive down the cost of labor too.

As a new person to Livestock business, you don't want to invest all your capital into buying lands in urban area which may turn out not being used because Government policy is against setting up poultry farm near residential/urban areas for health implication.

4. Investment Capital

1. With location in mind, you now have clearer idea of the capital required of you. Write down your detailed capital and investment requirements for your poultry farming in Nigeria venture and set out to source for it.

2. Like every other farming projects, the bigger you plan to start, the more investment required. You need to decide on the level of capital investment you are willing to commit into this business before starting.

3. Small scale Chicken Rearing (of about 50 birds) kept in cages at the backyard of your resident will take about ₦ 80, 000 to start.

4. A medium scale poultry farming that requires land and housing and other materials in 1– 2 plots of Land take about ₦ 1000, 000 to ₦ 2 Million to start.

Large scale or Intensive poultry farming that requires high level of sophistication and more careful planning and professionalism, using advance livestock farming techniques takes from ₦ 5 Million.

Develop Your Knowledge

The more business management tips and tricks you acquire, the more successful your poultry business will be. Poor business planning, results in poor farming management, and is the main factor that causes the failure of poultry farming, and small businesses in Nigeria. Learning about effective management of various areas, such as changing the food or water in the event of fecal contamination can lower the risk of disease.

In case of spillage of water, you can clean the areas, which have greater risk of breeding germs, and can result in your chickens becoming diseased, and potentially dying.

You should fully understand exactly what your chicken should eat. Feeding your chickens a complete and nutritious diet is essential if they are to stay healthy and lay lots of lovely profitable eggs! Chickens will eat almost anything, so, to prevent deficiencies and health problems, a wide range of foods should be offered. A good quality poultry pellet should be the mainstay of their diet. This can be supplemented with grains such as maize, soya cakes, groundnut, worms, insects and any other meat produce you can afford.

Poultry farming requires having the right knowledge to be able to do the right things to get the right result. It requires hard work and prompt attention to details. Poultry Farming is little capital intensive but if you are starting on a micro scale (Home back yard) where you have a small space at your back yard, it is not. Starting small is the best way to enter and learn the business.

Before you venture into poultry farming business in Nigeria and any other African country, you need to seat back and do proper planning; make sure you have an idea of all the costs involved.

Business plan is a very important part of every business venture and that is why you hear about it very often. Unfortunately, most people who think about starting a business usually don't consider writing a business plan.

I have read from different business experts about the fact that most start-up entrepreneurs do not write business plan but what I have not read from anyone is **why this is so.** Why is it that most people have fear (so to say) about writing a business plan?

I know the answer.

You see, there are many myths and lies you probably have heard about the subject of business plan. Some people present business plan as if it was a university thesis or an academic report to be defended before certain professors. Other people think that a business plan has to be 50 pages long and that it must be written in a certain "approved" format.

Well, I am here to tell you that all those opinions are not valid. Because there are some ugly lies around this important business step, most people are "afraid" of doing it

Journey with me as I will reveal the real truth about business plan, at the end you will discover that it is actually easy to write a business plan.

Why do you need a business plan?

There are three reasons why anyone may need a business plan.

First, if you`re about to start a business and you want to convince certain people to raise capital for you. In this case, you want to use your business plan to "sell" your business idea to the investors so they will be willing to finance your business.

Second, if you want to start a business and you`re willing to be successful. Though you don`t need external investors, you obviously need to grow, to compete and to win the battle of the market place. You need a business plan.

Third, you may need a new business plan because the economic or market situation has make your last plans obsolete. Yes, business plan is not like an academic paper which may stand for many years and still be relevant.

I wrote a business plan last year (I think April) and by December, it is already obsolete. Why? You really don`t know tomorrow. Your projections, plans or tactics are dependent on many factors that are beyond your power and when things change that affect your business (positively or negatively), then your plans also must be re-written.

How long should a business plan be and how many years should it be?

I am sure you know that my answer will not be in agreement with what you have been told before and the reason is because, you see, most people usually see the world we are as a **formal** world where everything has to be done formally.

That`s not true.

The world is <u>not</u> formal and every meaningful thing in the world is informal. Let me explain with an analogy.

If you are chatting with me on Face Book or WhatsApp, you will be looking at my profile picture and *assume* that you`re speaking with someone you`re seeing right in the profile picture. But no, the man who you`re seeing wears a good suit while the real me is wearing boxers and a signet. You think I am formal, but I am not.

How long should a business plan be?

Depending on your objective and who will read it. The last business plan I wrote was written on a single sheet of A4 paper. I typed and printed it out.

If you intend to write a business plan for yourself and not to convince any investor, I strongly recommend that you write your business plan in a single sheet of paper or two, worst, three.

I know this is a strange advice so let me explain.

You see, human nature loves complexity while simplicity is the only valuable thing. Anything that is too complex will give you stress and then become a burden on you, then you'll abandon it ... making it useless.

If you are planning to write a business plan for your own usefulness, you will have to review it often (or else you won't even follow it), so tell me, which document is easier to review, a ten pages document or two? You know the answer.

What if you want to write a business plan to convince the investors?

Some people will advise you to write 50 pages and some other entrepreneurs might have written 100 pages in the past, but let me tell you the truth, nobody has **time** to read your thesis except the university professors.

The only people who have so much time are the poor people and I am sure if at all you want to use your business plan to get an investor to finance your business, then you`re talking about someone who is (probably) very busy.

Let me tell you this so you will understand what I am saying here.

Many CV have been submitted to me by the job seekers in the past and I am sure they would have prepared those CVs thinking, "I will impress the employers". Well, here comes the sad news ... I have never in my life read a CV, I scan through them.

I don`t have time, please.

Your business plan is like the CV for the job seekers. How long should it be?

Its again depends on who will read it. 10 pages may help you. 15 pages may help you, but when you`re going beyond 20 pages, I am out!

If you forget everything, make sure you don`t forget this... the investors you will give your business plan to really don`t have time.

How many years should it be?

This area where people miss it; they write 5 or 10 year's business plan, I laugh!

Think about planning for your agribusiness the way you think about goals for your life.

When I first learned about goal setting, I was impressed by that idea and I started by writing 5 and 10 years goals. I was wrong.

It never worked. I later started writing one year goal and now I am writing goal for a third of the year (4 months). The reason is simple... you`re a human being like all of us. What you think/plan that will happen will not happen the way you plan it.

Any agribusiness plan that is more than one year is actually questionable. That is my opinion. Any other business expert may tell you something different.

So what and what should your plan contain? Before answering this question, permit me to cross out a popular lie about business plan.

Most people believe that if your plan is well written, it will win you huge amount of money from the investors. This is like telling a graduate, hey, if you can write your CV very well, you will be employed in a big company.

That was then. I hate certificate and CV and every single time people have submitted them to me, I have asked myself, what can this man/woman render as value for us (as organization)?

Do you think I am the only one with this mindset? Do you think your intending investors will be bought by a super-written plan? Think again.

Most investors will rather judge your five sentences than your 50 pages plans. That doesn't mean that you shouldn't write your plan very well. It simply means that you have more to do than just writing a plan.

You have to understand in and out, front and back, up and down of your intending

Agribusiness. In fact, **the written plan is nothing but the abstract of what is in your head,** or else, you`ll fail in your attempt to convince business partners or investors to help your agribusiness.

Some people believe that business plan is what anyone (an expert) can sit down somewhere and just write for them. A man called me about two months ago and that was what he wanted me to do for him.

If I write a "superb" plan for you, will I still be the one to defend it when your investors ask you questions? That is why the first task you have is to understand your agribusiness very well.

Okay, now let me tell you seven things that your business plan should contain. I will not write any complex term or academic jargon here (because I believe the world is not complex)

1. Your business name/title.

This is obvious. For example, Lenarc-phil Poultry Farm`s Business Plan

2. Objective/summary.

They call this Executive Summary, but don't be deceived by this name. It simply means, *why you are writing this plan.*

What do you want to achieve with your plan? If you're giving it to an investor, what do you want from him?

Constructively state your objective here. If you're giving your plan to someone you want to convince to partner with you, state your objective and if your intention is to get him to finance your agribusiness venture, state that here.

3. Business description.

What and what is your agribusiness all about? What is your farming all about? What are the future possibilities and threats in your farm? Describe your intending agribusiness here.

4. Market strategy

An investor expects you to have been familiar with your product/service and market, as close as you are to your wife.

He wants you to convince him of your intending marketing strategies and that is the reason for this face. How do you intend to win a good market share for your produce?

This is very important, even if you`re not presenting your plan to any investor. In the business terminology, they will advise you to conduct a **market analysis.**

I hate to use big grammar.

What that simply means is that you should spend time to research and understand your market, then position yourself with the tactics to win. That`s what an investor wants you to tell him here.

5. Competitors` analysis.

Here, an investor will want you to convince him that you understand the strengths and weaknesses of your competitors. Some people come up with a formula they call SWORT analysis.

It simply means that you should analyses the **S**trengths, **W**eaknesses, **O**pportunity, **R**eward and the **T**hreats in the market place. This will help you to know how to play your agribusiness game and if you`ll be presenting your business plan to an investor, this will encourage him that you actually understand your "enemies" and are able to ~~kill them in~~ the business for you to succeed

6. Your people.

If I want to invest with you, won't I have interest in knowing who and who will be part of your agribusiness team? That is what you will want to write here. Who will be doing what, who will be handle what and who will be employed later to take care of what? These are the answers you have to provide here.

7. Financial situations and forecasts.

Here you`ll want to write about the financial requirements of your agribusiness, amount on ground now and what and what is needed to run the business successful in future.

Above you have it. A guide that can help you to write a good agribusiness plan, and you see, all I have written here are by no means a "standard formula".

Chapter 2

Have Your Investment Ready

Poultry farming requires investment. You can arrange the money by your own or you can apply for bank loan. Both government and non-government bank loans are available for starting poultry farming business. You should contact your desired bank for the loan process. As a beginner, you should start with a minimum number of birds which will cost you pretty less money. I will discuss more about getting funds to start this business in this chapter.

How much do I need to start a poultry farm?

In one hand, I would have loved to compare your intending poultry venture to giving birth to many children. You will have to feed them, cloth them and house them, plus give them proper medications... all these methodically.

And to be candid, if you`re not willing to take care of your chickens as you`ll your children, maybe you should not start a chicken farm at all.

I remember then when I was managing my parent`s poultry alongside with them. Really,

They were our "children".

The Cost of Starting a Poultry Farm

If you`re a beginner on this business, you definitely have interest in this question.

However, as much as I will love to give you a straight answer here, there is no straight answer.

Do you know? What a farmer uses to acquire land alone may be what another person will use to start and run a profitable poultry business. Land, which is one of the major expenses you will incur, is varying in price. This depends on location.

What you have to do is to make your findings.

Every other instruments, feeds and medications you will need is vary too, depending on where you are living, so don`t let me make any futile guess that may confuse you. This is what I want you to do. Make a list of everything you`ll need (from land to the littlest vaccine) and move out to investigate their prices in your vicinity. I know you may not know what and what you will need (since I've assumed you don`t know anything about poultry farming business), so below I will make a list of what and what you will need.

1.   Land/space. This depends on your intending scale (I mean size of your farm). What if you have a large space at your backyard? It may be good to start with in a small scale.

2.   A waste disposal system. Where will you be disposing the waste from your farm?

3.   A clean source of water. I mean clean (I have told you that you`ll have to take care of your birds like children)

4.   Lighting and heat will be needed.

5.   Storage space for keeping your birds` foods, vaccines and eggs.

6.   Those things you see them putting chicken`s food on.

7.   Where they drink from.

8.   Nests

9.   Perches

10.   Egg trays or crates

11.   Vaccines and food which could be your major expenses

12.   Honestly, I might have missed a few things here but when you visit the retailers who deal in these equipment you`ll be reminded. **Also in Chapter 9:** Purchase Required Equipment, I will talk more on the equipments you need.

Before you start your poultry farming business, it is important that you have enough details on the cost implication of the project. I have seen many people jump at such projects without having enough details of what it would cost them and along the line; they end up frustrated when they find out that the start-up cost is more than they bargained or prepared for.

In order to avoid this type of problem, it is important that you read this chapter thoroughly and also carry out a personal research of your own; so that you can have full details on the costs of setting up your poultry farm.

First, you have to decide if you want to set up a small scale poultry farm or a very large one. This is the first factor that would determine your start-up cost. For instance, if you want to set up a backyard poultry farm, you may not need to spend too much money.

You will probably just need to build a good cage for the birds, provide a good feeding and water drinking system and then provide some warmth and security for the birds. But if you want to go into large scale poultry farming, you would need a whole lot of materials, equipment and tools. Some of the things you would need include-:

1. Land

First, you would need to purchase a good plot of land that would be suitable for farming. Farm lands are usually cheaper than lands in residential areas, so you may be lucky to get a very sizable plot at a very good price.

In Nigeria for instance, you can get a very good plot of farm land with about N300, 000. I am certain that regardless of which county you decide to set up your poultry farm, you should be able to get a good farmland within the price range of ₦ 250, 000 and ₦ 500, 000 or even cheaper.

2. Construction Costs:

The next stage after purchase of land is construction. You would have to build a cage to keep the birds in. There are different types of cages and you can check one in Chapter 5 on how to start a poultry farm for the different types of poultry housing.

When you have decided on the most suitable one for you, then you can call in experts to give you a quote but using Nigeria as a case study, then I will say a good poultry housing alone would cost you nothing less than N150,000 but it still depends on the size of your poultry farm. You may also need to construct some building like stores for keeping equipment and supplies and maybe a security/farm house for farm laborers.

3. Chicks

The next thing you would have to spend on is getting chicks to start your farm with. As a beginner, you wouldn't have chicks of your own yet so you would have to buy from other poultry farmers. The number of chicks you would need depends on the size of your farm and the capacity of the poultry housing you have constructed.

The price would also depend on the size of the chicks. Day old chicks are usually very cheap and one chick cost between N120 - N250 depending on the period of the purchase. You may even get it for cheaper but you have to be careful when handling day old chicks because they are usually at a high risk of dying.

4. Poultry Equipment

This is yet another thing that is dependent on the size of your poultry farm and the nature of your business. If you want to hatch and sell chicks for instance, you would have to buy hatchery equipment. If you want to process meat for sale, you would also need meat processing equipment. The same thing goes for if you want to produce your own poultry feed yourself.

So as for cost of equipment, you would really have to sit down and decide on the nature of poultry farming you want to do and find out the type of equipment you would need.

5. Vaccination

Your birds must be given the necessary medical attention so that they can grow properly and produce efficiently. You have to include the costs of vaccination in your business plan. This cost would also include costs of drugs and payment to the medical consultant that would be called upon to give the birds the required medical attention. Again, you should have a budget of at least N5, 000 for about 200 birds.

6. Feeding

This is like the most important expense you would undertake in this business. Feeding is very important because the growth and productivity of your birds would depend on how well you feed them. There are different types of poultry feeds for different stages in the bird's lives.

There is the starter or chick mash for birds when they are little chicks, there is the grower for optimal growth and strength and there is the finisher and layers for when they are getting close to the selling or egg laying stage. You can budget about 70 percent of the total expenses depending on the type of birds you intend to keep and how for how long. For 200 chicks, you can budget about N140,000 but if you want to cut costs of feeding, you can consider producing your own poultry feed. Although this may cost you a lot of money for a start, it would save you a lot of money in the long run. I will teach you how to make your own poultry feed in chapter 9.

7. Cost of Labor

If you are setting up a commercial poultry farm, it is unlikely that you would be capable of handling all the tasks yourself. You may have to employ people to assist you and you would need to pay them. You can make a budget of at least N100, 000 for that but the actual cost would depend on labor rates in the country where you want to set up your poultry farm.

8. Other Expenses

You should also make out a budget for electricity, transportation, advertising, security, insurance as well as selling and distribution expenses.

To get a detailed and accurate cost of setting up your poultry farm, it is advisable for you to carry out your own feasibility study.

How to Finance Your Poultry Business Start-up, Growth or Acquisition

Over the years of running my Agribusiness and interacting with other business owners / aspiring entrepreneurs, I have come to understand the fact that raising capital will remain the most challenging task for an entrepreneur.

You may have the most brilliant idea in the world, or you have mapped out a formidable expansion plan for your existing business; however, if you cannot raise the needed funds to pursue these ideas or plans, nothing will ever get done.

There are three components to starting an agribusiness. One is the right plan; two is the right team and three is the money. Rarely do these three components come together when starting a business. It's the duty of an entrepreneur to grab one piece and start the business, the remaining two pieces will be found along the way. Finding the remaining two components may take a year or more than a year; the point is, start with what you have.

Getting funds to start a new business (*or expand an existing one*) is one of the most difficult challenges you can ever face as an entrepreneur. This is because most of the widely known sources of funding (*such as bank loans and venture capital*) are highly competitive; running after them is like racing with many other cars on an extremely crowded highway. That is, many businesses, both small and big are fighting hard to get funds from these same sources.

Now, I am not saying you cannot get bank loans or venture capital. But the bitter truth is, you will most likely have to fight through all the clutter for several weeks to months just to get your voice heard. Moreover, your poultry business may not be ripe for these funds, as they are usually reserved for companies that have already reached certain milestones. Yet, only with the needed funds can your business reach those milestones.

So, *what should you do rather than waste months to years trying to get funds from these tight sources*? The answer is to avoid the highly competitive options. Instead of racing with other cars on the jammed highway, you can choose to take the side streets (*provided you can easily navigate your way through them*).

Preparing Yourself for the Challenges of Raising Capital

Raising capital for your startup or funds for your small business expansion plans is no doubt one of the most challenging aspects of starting or growing a business. This is why you must be adequately prepared for the task.

Seriously, raising money for your poultry business is not a piece of cake; as you almost have to practically beg and convince potential investors or lenders to trust you with their hard earned money. There are more-than-countable stories of entrepreneurs and small business owners becoming discouraged and frustrated by the harsh challenges they are faced with while trying to raise funds for their businesses.

"Getting rich begins with the right mindset, the right words and the right plan."

These challenges include the amount of time it takes to secure the required funds, the crippling terms and conditions, the paper work involved, the rejections, and the lack of linearity and progress checkpoints over the course of the fund raising process. Now, let us go into more detail on some of the commonest challenges entrepreneurs face during the fund raising process.

Common Challenges of Entrepreneurs during the Funding Raising Process

1. The "*maybe*" situation

It is very common for a prospective investor, either an individual or a venture firm to show great interest in an entrepreneur's idea after the initial review, only to leave the entrepreneur guessing afterwards by not giving any definitive feedback (*positive or negative*) on the investment proposition. No entrepreneur would find this an easy experience.

Because they "*have the gold*" and "make the rules," investors demand that you, being the entrepreneur, provide a very specific timeline in regards to growth metrics and return on their prospective investment. But they usually don't reciprocate this by making quick and specific investment decisions. Why should they be hasty about investing in your business, when there are other promising business opportunities out there?

2. Lack of urgency

Another great challenge in raising funds for a new or existing business is the lack of natural urgency. This is usually because the number of entrepreneurs seeking to market their ideas by far exceeds that of ready investors. And so, investors have their tables filled with several investment proposals and usually need enough time to go through them and scrutinize the opportunities that each one presents.

"The rich invest in time, the poor invest in money." – **Warren Buffett**

Also, most investors / lenders are busy individuals with many corporate and personal issues to attend to; thus leaving them with less time to go through the numerous business plans they receive daily. So get their attention, your business plan and email pitch must be exceptional and attention grabbing.

With the above in mind, let's now look at the qualities you must have in order to cope with the various challenges involved in the fund raising process. These following qualities will help you level the playing field, mitigate the balance of power, and accelerate the fundraising process.

Qualities You Need to Successfully Raise Startup Fund

What are the basic traits possessed by successful fund raisers. Every entrepreneur knows that there's more to raising funds than simply stretching out your hand to ask for money. To successfully raise capital, there are certain traits, characteristics or qualities that you must possess. Your ability to develop and use these traits tactically will go a long way to determine if you will get the money you need or not.

In this write up, I will be highlighting the basic qualities or traits you need to succeed in the game of small business financing and fund raising. I will also point out the exact way each trait can benefit you in your quest to raise money.

1. Strong determination

"Without passion, you don't have energy. Without energy, you have nothing." – Warren Buffett.

This is the most important quality that you need to succeed in your fund raising quest. Without strong determination, you would quickly give up after facing one or two of the harrowing challenges that accompany the process.

"Passion keeps you going, when the going gets tough." – **Warren Buffett**

Determination is a product of passion and self-belief. When you are passionate about what you do and you strongly belief in the workability of your product, determination follows. Determination toughens your skin towards rejection, it keeps your eyes fixed on your long-term goals and blinded to the harsh challenges that you will encounter along the way. It helps you stay on track and fuels you with optimism.

2. Patience

"Patience; this is the greatest business asset. Wait for the right time to make your moves."

– J. Paul Getty.

As stated earlier, some investors or loan-issuing institutions could be very annoying. They may take too long to review and respond to your proposal, leaving you to fall sick of suspense and anxiety. Worse, they may reject your proposal for flimsy reasons even after showing great enthusiasm initially.

As far as raising funds for your business is concerned, you are at the mercy of these investors or loan-issuers; even though you own the business idea or concept. This is more true especially when you are a first time entrepreneur without much business experience or track record. So, you must be ready to play along with them if you really want to succeed.

"The world belongs to the patient man." – The Mafia Manager

Some investors would eventually buy your idea after making you believe that your business idea is not worth a dime; or doing all sorts of things that would make you think they are not interested. You never can tell what an investor's final decision would be. So, don't blow your chances by acting or reacting unprofessionally. Give potential investors or creditors all the time they need to make a decision that satisfies them.

"If you are the anvil, be patient. If you are the hammer; strike." – The Mafia Manager

Also, you should never try to force your idea down an investor's throat, as this will send wrong signals that may make them nurse doubts over your idea. If your idea is promising, you will get the funds you need. If you get a negative response, then take it in good faith. It may not necessarily mean that your idea isn't good. It may be because the investor or creditor doesn't just have enough funds to pump into your idea, or your idea is in his / her industry of competence.

3. Business sense

"To succeed in business, to reach the top, an individual must know all that is possible to know about that business." – J. Paul Getty

The next trait investors look out for in entrepreneurs seeking funding is passion and core competence. No investor / lender would want to put money in a fly-by-night idea; they want to put money in a business that the entrepreneur is truly passionate about. Most importantly, investors / lenders want to put money in a business where you, the entrepreneur is willing to work for free; at least to some certain extent.

Also, you must be very knowledgeable about the business you are raising funds for. In fact, you must know your business industry like the back of your hand; that even if you are awakened from sleeps and questioned about your business, you will deliver without stuttering.

"See thou a man diligent in his business? He shall stand before kings; he shall not stand before vain men." – Proverbs 22: 29

4. Your sales skills

"The ability to sell is the number one skill in business. If you cannot sell, don't bother thinking about becoming a business owner." – Rich Dad

The last and most important key to your fund raising success is your ability to sell, and this prevails over most other factors. Now *why must you learn how to sell*? Selling is a crucial skill that you must have as an entrepreneur, and this is because when it comes to raising funds, the commonest question on the lips or in the minds of investors and creditors is, *"What are you selling?"*

In addition to introducing your business idea and your plans for actualizing it, you must be able to explain how the investor or creditor will gain from the deal. Investors want a healthy return on their investment. And though they know you cannot be 100% accurate, they want an estimate of how much profit they will get back from the business if they invest their money.

To up your chances of getting the funds you need, you must be able to brilliantly present the business model as well as its profitability. This is why sales, persuasion and presentation skills are very important to the fund raising process if you are raising funds from investors, friends and relatives.

6 ways of raising money for Poultry Agribusiness

It's almost unanimous, the number one problem facing everyone before starting farming or any other business is CAPITAL! I have highlighted below some of the ways you can get money to start your agribusiness.

1. Bank Loans

The most common way people get capital to finance their enterprise is through bank loans. You open an account with a bank of your choice, have it operational for a minimum of six months and you are good to go! You will be given a loan depending on the amount of money you have been banking monthly at your bank.

Unfortunately since most youths or graduates do not have an income to deposit regularly in a bank I have a solution that can still help you get a loan from your bank. If you completely don't have any source of income or capital for farming you can look for at least ten people (this is the minimum number of people to form a youth group in Nigeria) you know, who are aged between 18-35 years and form a youth group (Youth group registration services are done at your states local area council centers all over Nigeria). By doing this your youth group can easily get funding from banks by raising only 30 % of the money being asked for.

2. Government Youth Funding

The Nigerian Government has launched various funding programmes that have been designed to specifically target the youth. Individuals though have to meet certain requirements for them to be eligible for funding. These funding solutions can therefore go a long way in jumpstarting your farming business.

3. Family and Friends

One good source of business financing that is often overlooked is money from relatives and friends. A gift is one of the simplest ways of getting capital for a business. A friend or family member might decide to offer you a gift of money to help out start a business or you might initiate the process by asking. Though asking your friend or family member for a gift of money may seem impolite, when it's a startup business, it can make sense.

4. Business Loans from Family and Friends

You can also ask for money from a friend or family member with a promise to pay it back. It's usually in accordance with certain terms and can be done with interest or without interest. After asking for the money you promise to pay it back, over a set time period, and in accordance with certain terms. For the sake of friendship and family ties it is always best to handle this kind of loan the same way a bank would. This means it has to include a signed agreement which is called a promissory note and a time period you will pay back the loan.

5. Equity Investors

This is another way you can raise money to start a business. This method gives you the opportunity is to give away part of your business to an "equity investor." An equity investor can either be a friend or a family member. This will make you co-owners and thus share any net profits or losses generated by your business.

6. Savings

The urban lifestyle in Nigeria has convinced the youth that they don't have money. Save that 5000 naira you spend every weekend to party. For youth seriously interested in farming, saving this money for 3 weeks will be enough capital to set up some small-scale poultry business or any other agribusiness. Students in colleges and universities receive allowances from their parents, those who receive government grants are even better placed to invest this money and reap the benefits when they graduate. Sadly many students prefer to buy the latest gadgets and indulge in weekly (or daily) drinking escapades.

In conclusion, raising money to start your agribusiness isn`t hard. You only need to think creatively on how to get funds and also I always advise that you start small then expand your business slowly.

Chapter 3

Poultry Production Type

First of all determine the production type of your poultry farm. You can raise broiler chickens for meat production purpose and choose layers if you want to produce eggs commercially. You can also start your poultry farm for selling poultry products and breeding stocks directly to your local customers. Determine your production purpose, select proper poultry breeds according to your desired production and go for the detailed planning.

Which is more profitable? Layers, Broilers or Indigenous breed

In the chicken industry in Nigeria, there are three main sectors: Layers, which are chickens bred raised to produce eggs, or broilers, chickens raised and bred to be slaughtered for meat and the indigenous breeds. Whatever sector you choose, you have to make the right decisions to make your chicken business a profitable one.

I have come across the question of which is the best enterprise between broilers and layers on several different occasions. I will not give a direct answer. However our team did a simple calculation to help you make a decision. Please follow and ask questions if you don't understand.

1.   The calculation below is based on feeds only since it contributes to up to 70% of cost of production and does not cover costs of drugs, or building or labour and other overheads.

2.   It is based on current market price which changes from time to time and should be used as a guide.

Feeding cost for 500 Broiler birds depending on the bread for 10 weeks

☐   0 – 4 weeks. 30 bags of 25kg of Broiler starter costs N108, 000 at N3600 per 25kg bag of feed for the first 4 weeks.

☐   5-8 weeks. 40 bags of Broiler finisher costs N140, 000 at N3500 per 25kg bag of feed for the remaining next 4 weeks.

Now you can sale at this stage but if you desire to rear them for 10 weeks depending on your market demand,

☐ 9-10 weeks. 30 bags of Broiler finisher feed sold at N105, 000 at N3500 per 25 kg bag of feed for the next one week.

☐ Maximum amount of broiler starter given to chicks in 4 weeks is N108,000

☐ Maximum amount of broiler finisher feed fed to mature birds for 6 weeks is

☐ N245,000

☐ Total bags of 25kg feed given for 10 weeks are 100.

☐ Total Cost of feeding of Broiler for 10 weeks = N 353,000

☐ Cost of buying day old broiler chick depending on the breed and season, N220 per chick. Multiply by 500. It will amount to N110, 000.

☐ Total cost of feeds = N 353,000 + N 110,000 = **N 463,000**

☐ Revenue from Sale of 500 birds at N2000 = **N 100,000,000**

☐ Gross Margin = N 537, 000.

Now remember this is not your profit per say. You need to add the cost of vaccines and medication, water, labour other over head expenses before you arrive at your profit.

The cob 700 is the most efficient breed available at the time of writing this book, while marshal is known for been tall and heavy weight. The season of your sale also can positively influence your returns.

Note: If you what to make good money with broiler and Indigenous breed hens, you need to learn how to formulate and produce feed by yourself instead of buying packed feed from companies. I will educate you more about it at chapter 9.

Feeding cost for 500 Layers birds

☐   Chick mash @ N 45/kg fed from wk 1 to wk 8

☐   Growers mash @ N 30/kg fed from wk 9 to wk 19

☐   Layers mash @ N 40/kg fed from wk 20 to wk 84

☐   One tray of egg sold for N 320.

<u>NOTE</u>

1.   Maximum amount of feed fed to chicks per day = 60g

2.   Maximum amount of feed fed to growers per day=90g

3.   Maximum amount of feed fed to layers per day=120g

❖ Cost of feeding Chick mash = N 75,600

❖ Cost of feeding growers mash = N 103,950

❖ Cost of feeding layers mash = N 1,092,000

❖ Total Feed costs = N 1,271,550

❖ Revenue from sale of eggs

❖ Laying percentage =85%

❖ Total eggs collected for 455 days =193,375

Total crates = 6446 × N 320 (cost of one crate) Total revenue = N 2,062,720

Gross margin = N 970,720 Profit per Month = 51,090

Conclusion

1.   Therefore rearing layers is profitable in the long run, i.e. in the two years.

2.   You need to plan before investing in layers as your hens will stay for up to 18 weeks before starting laying, meaning no revenue at the beginning.

3.   Hen can lay continuously up 2 years with average percentage of 85%

4.   Broilers reach market weight after 2 months.

Also I must say that all breeds (Indigenous breed, layers and broilers). I have seen farmers make a lot of money from each breed. How? Their passion and skills of rearing each type of breed has made them succeed. I will talk more about each breed in the next chapters.

Chapter 4

Broiler Hens

Broiler poultry farming is a lucrative business. Generally highly meat productive birds or poultry breeds are called broiler poultry. But broiler chicken is a special species of poultry, which is a great secret. Only four countries of the world know about this secret and they supply and maintain all the demand of broiler chickens. Broilers are like other common poultry birds. But this broiler is made in a scientific way for producing more meat in a short time. Basically, broilers are only for meat production.

Many people are interested in broilers farming. Broilers are meat birds often referred to as fryers in some places. They are bred to grow fast so that they are ready for the dinner table between 6 and 10 weeks of age. Currently in Nigeria there seems to be a huge demand for broilers which may not be satisfied any time soon. But the catch is to know the market, i.e. whom are you producing for?

Broilers are sold between 1.5 and 3kg live weight depending on consumers' preferences and market demands. Finding out the market outlets should be the first task before investing in broiler production. You ought to make marketing arrangements with local hotels, restaurants, cafeterias, groceries, and other regular users before rearing broilers for sale. This will ensure timely and regular orders for the birds and that no birds are left unsold.

Sell graded or classified birds because proper grading or classification attracts different types of consumers. This will also enable the consumers to make purchasing decision on bird size at hand. Broilers are judged on cleanliness and the valuable meat areas i.e. large breasts and thighs. They should also be appealing when dressed out, which means they should not have any skin imperfections or broken wing feathers. After dressing place them in seal bags and only show the broilers that look perfect.

Don't forget to keep records of your expenses. It may cost more to raise broilers than to buy them at the supermarket, but the recreation and satisfaction derived offset the higher cost. In addition, manure and litter from broiler production can be used as organic manure.

Selecting Broiler for Business

There are many breeds of broiler. Before selecting broilers for business the farmer have to maintain some process. Those important steps are described below.

☐   The broiler chick of one day should weigh between 36 to 40 grams.

☐   It is found that if the baby chick of one day old becomes good weight then it will give great return when you will sell them.

☐   To get more and affordable benefits from broiler poultry farming the farmer should select the good and high productive breeds for business.

☐   As broiler convert food to meat so provide them high quality food.

☐ The farmer has to ensure high ratio of protein and calorie in broiler chicken food.

☐ For the chicken of 0-6 weeks the food should contain 22.24% protein and 2900-3000 metabolic heat.

☐ Among the amino acid, lysine and methionine is very essential and important in broiler poultry food. Because this acids helps to enhance chicken health, and help to convert food to meat.

☐ In broiler food the ratio of fiber should not be more than 6 percent.

☐ Vitamin A, B2, D3, B12 and K are extensive requirements to broiler food.

☐ Potassium, Iodine, Manganese Sulphate and Zinc carbonate should mixed well separately and feed the chicken.

☐ A little amount of disinfectant should mix in broiler food and this will keep the chick free from diseases.

NOTE: More shall be discussed in the later chapters.

Housing

The broiler house should be placed east-west direction. Ventilation system must be well accompanied. The regular distance from one house to another house will be 11-12 meters (35-40 feet). The house should be cleaned well before bringing the chick to the farm. The insects like lice, mosquito, etc should run off with blow lamp. Heating system of the space of baby chicken should be observed well 24 hours before the chick reach the farm. The temperature of the house should 35 degree centigrade. 7 square inch of space per chick is required. Always keep a moderate number of chicks; it will keep the chicken healthy. You will learn more about housing in Chapter 5.

Feed and Water

Proper and high quality feed is the main thing to success in broiler poultry farming. Broiler poultry consume feed and convert them to meat. So, to be success the farmer should be conscious of feed management. Broiler poultry needs high ratio of protein in their feed to grow well. They should also provide proper vitamin like A, B2, D3, B12 and K to meet their needs.

Provide some disinfectant to keep them free from poultry diseases. Broiler poultry eats feed and water whole day and night. So, make sure the supply of feed and water all time. Along with feed, fresh and clean water is very important. Broiler poultry takes a lot of water every day. Make the water available all time to their cage. In winter season farmer should supply warm water. However, to be successful the farmer must have to be more careful in feed and water management. We will discuss details about broiler poultry feed and water management later in chapter 9.

☐ For the first few days you can serve feed in egg carton.

☐ 2.5 cm space is required per chick until they reach 1 week.

☐ For the first time you can fill the feeder fully, but don't do that when they grow enough. It reduces the food waste.

☐ Provide the feed four times a day.

☐ Provide fresh and clean water all time.

☐ Water pot should keep as much as possible according to the number of chicken.

☐ You have to keep in mind that broiler takes more water than layer chicken. The broiler chicken takes more water in summer season.

Temperature

Temperature is very important in broiler poultry farming. You should check the temperature of the broiler chicken house 48 hours before bringing the chick to the farm. For the first week the temperature of the rood would be 35° C and it will reduce at the rate 2.80°c per week, it mostly depend on the outside temperature. The litter of the chicken would between 5-6 inch depth. If possible keep some straw in the chicken bed. The chicken bed should clean twice a week with spade. If the condition of the bed is very wet then you can use lime because it absorbs the ammonia gas.

Broiler Chicken Startup Light Touch

The process of rearing broilers can be a sensitive affair from the time you get them from the distributors/hatchery when they are 1day old chicks until they reach maturity.

For any kind of animal husbandry the work always starts prior to the animal even reaching the farm and for chicken it's no different.

STEP 1: The Brooder

Before you go and get your chicks, you should first ensure that you have adequately prepared the brooder. *A brooder is a farm structure specifically constructed for chicks with special attention to temperature control and proper hygiene.*

Temperature control is important for day old chicks because they do not have the 'mother hen' to shelter them from the cold and they do not have feathers and instead have a fur like covering. Without a source of heat for the chicks the mortality rate goes up and one risks losing the entire lot.

Temperature control can be achieved through two main ways:

☐   Use of ***poultry gas heater*** – this involves using the gas burner specially constructed by Lenarc-phil technologies Nig. Ltd for providing heat for the newly arrived chicks

☐   Use of **mercury bulbs** – which are special bulbs designed to produce heat.

Please note that care should be taken when adjusting how low the mercury bulb should hang. If it's too high then the chicks will hurdle together and the ones in the bottom will suffocate and die. If it's too low some chicks may die of heat stroke. A good indicator of how low to hang the bulb is through observing how the chicks react to the heat, if they hurdle together, lower the bulb a bit lower but if some move away to far corners then raise the bulb because it's too low. See a mercury bulb on the image below:

Below are the chicks in the night with the light on:

STEP 2

Care should be taken when transporting day old chicks especially when using a car it is important to make sure the vehicle is well ventilated and that the chicks are not stacked up to the extent that some have no access to fresh air.

STEP 3

With day old chicks it is advisable to start them off immediately on anti-stress vitamins to help them cope with the sudden change in environment. Common anti-stress vitamins in the market include: Aliseryl, Vitalyte, Egocin and Agrar [if un-available agro vets can always advise you on a good substitute]

You can also mix the vitamin water with some glucose and glycerine. The glucose gives the chicks energy and keeps them active increasing the speed of their metabolism so that they can eat more and develop faster. The glycerine [in small portions] helps 'smoothen' the chicks' intestines aiding them in excretion of their waste.

Below is a sample of vitamin water mix; you can as well mix other meds or vaccines in there.

STEP 4

For broilers, you have the starter meal and the finisher meal. The starter meal is a mash made up of finely ground maize, fish, millet and sorghum mixed together. This meal is specifically for day old chicks because it is easy on their delicate digestive systems and it is advisable to keep the chicks on this meal for at least the first 2wks.

After the first 2wks the chicks ought to have developed feathers and you can thus move them from the brooder to the main chicken house and can change the meal to finishers mash or pellets. The major difference between the finisher mash/pellets and the starter mash is that the finisher mash is not as finely ground as the starters mash which is understandable because at this time their digestive system is well developed and can handle the heavier feeds.

You can keep the broilers on the finisher's meal [**being fed 3times a day**] for 4wks – 5wks before they reach maturity and can be sold.

STEP 5: VACCINES & VITAMINS

Below is a schedule of the vaccines needed to reduce mortality rate for broilers:

☐   After 1wk – Newcastle vaccine

☐   After 2wks – Infectious Bursal Disease (Gumboro) scientific names: [Bur 706, TAD, Hipra(IBD)]

☐   After 3wks – Newcastle vaccine

☐   After 4wks – Gumboro vaccine

The above vaccines are administered via the chicken's drinking water. In order to ensure that they take the vaccine it is advisable to deny the chicken water for about 6hrs depending on the season to make sure they are thirsty before giving them the vaccinated water.

OTHER USEFUL TIPS

☐ Maintain a Monitoring & Evaluation – This will help comparing one lot to the next and help identify areas that need improvement.

☐ Have a well-defined/regular feeding pattern – This will make sure the animals are not 'stressed' and weight progress is even

☐ Make sure the chicken house floor is always dry – This will reduce chances of bacterial or viral infections.

☐ Disinfect the brooder 1-2 weeks before introducing the day old chicks. This is the same for the main poultry house; disinfect it 1-2 weeks before bringing in the chicks from the brooder.

☐ Make sure the brooder/poultry house is well light during the day and night. This encourages the chicks/chicken to keep feeding and hence attain the required weight in time.

☐ Ensure the structure is well aerated.

THE ONLY EQUIPMENTS ARE:

You will need:

1.   Feeding troughs. There are several options, choose the best for you.

2.   Drinkers: either plastic or metallic drinkers. Plastics are easy to clean and can last longer

3.   Enough lighting during the night. You may prefer having electric power available or solar.

4.   A brooder for the day old chicks. A brooder can be within the main poultry house by simply curving out a place for the chicks and removing the guides as the chicks attain 2wks. For a professional brooder it would need to off the ground and separated from the main house.

Poultry gas heater or heat-generating electric bulbs within the brooder to maintain enough heat within the brooder during the night or during cold day times.

Chapter 5

Layers Hens

Layer poultry farming means raising egg laying poultry birds for the purpose of commercial egg production, Layer chickens are such a special species of hens, which need to be raised from when they are one day old. They start laying eggs commercially from 18-19 weeks of age.

They remain laying eggs continuously till their 72-78 weeks of age. They can produce about one kg of eggs by consuming about 2.25 kg of food during their egg laying period. For the purpose of producing hybrid eggs layer, consider the various characteristics of cock and hen before breeding. There are various types of highly egg productive layer breeds available throughout the world.

Layer Breeds

According to the nature and color of egg, layer hens are of two types. Short descriptions of these two types are listed below.

1. White Egg Laying Hens:

This type of hens is comparatively smaller in size. Relatively eat less food, and the color of egg shell is white. Isa White, Lehman White, Nikchik, Bab Cock BV-300, Havard White, Hi Sex White, Sever White, Hi line White, Bovanch White etc. are some popular white egg laying chickens.

2. Brown Egg Laying Hens

Brown egg laying hens are relatively larger in size. They eat more foods, compared to white egg layers. Lay bigger eggs than other laying breeds. Egg shell is brown colored. There are many types of brown layer available. Among those Isa Brown, Hi Sex Brown, Sever 579, Lehman Brown, Hi Line Brown, Bab Cock BV-380, Gold Line, Bablona Tetro, Bablona Harko, Havard Brown etc. are very suitable for commercial layer poultry farming.

Layer Hen Selection

You have to keep in mind some essential information before selecting the layer hens for your poultry farming business. You have to select those breeds which are suitable for your layer poultry farming business and can produce well in your area. Read below for selecting proper breeds for your business.

☐   For commercial eggs production, you have to choose highly productive laying hens correctly.

☐   All type of hens do not produce equal number of eggs.

☐   The chosen breeds must have to have good production capability.

☐   If your chosen breed contains the desired characteristic and have a reputation for egg production, then that breed is suitable for your business.

☐   Always purchase healthy chicks from a famous and popular hatchery. You can see their catalog before purchasing and demand for the vaccine schedule of the breed.

We will talk more about chick selection and highly laying breeds.

Keeping Chicks

During the first weeks after birth, many chicks do not want to drink water due to transporting them from one place to another. So you have to make adequate water drinking systems in their brooder house, and you have to train them for drinking water. Mix 5% glucose with water, so that they can easily get energy.

Provide them with any types of high quality multivitamin by mixing with water (suggested by electrolyte Production Company's instruction). Multivitamin and electrolyte are very effective when you transport chick from a long distance. It reduces tiredness and lack of water, and help to make the chick normal. I will explain more in chapter 9.

Chick Vaccination Programme

Vaccination and its Importance

Many poultry diseases can be prevented by good management practices, including sanitation, adequate feeding, well-ventilated houses, etc. However, some poultry diseases, particularly viral and bacterial disease, could easily and rapidly spread, and can result in a high death toll. The most reasonable approach to the control of these diseases is by vaccination. You have to maintain some rules before vaccination.

- ❖ To protect is better than curing. An adage that has its full interpretation as far as poultry business is concern. The effect of diseases outbreak is life lasting in poultry.
  - ❖ Birds will hardly reach their original designed potential once they suffer am outbreak.
  - ❖ Vaccination is the only way out. No substitute for sound vaccinations. If there is no money for feed in none-laying birds or in a broiler farm, you can skip a day without feed. It is safer than failure to vaccinate.
  - ❖ Use anti-stress or vitamins/mineral mix for 2 days before and after vaccination.
  - ❖ Use powdered milk to de-chlorinate water giving water soluble vaccines only water (chemically tested) with no chlorine will require no milk make sure two weeks elapsed between the first and second Gumboro. Also provide adequate number of drinkers when giving vaccine in water to avoid overdosing and or under dosing. Re suggest that you provide one plastic drinker for every 25 birds.
  - ❖ Don't over excite birds within the period of vaccination.
  - ❖ Do not change house immediately after vaccination.
  - ❖ Immediately after any vaccination, give birds water with some common salt in it. Use it at a dose of I gram per liter of water or 1 teaspoonful into a gallon of water.

- ❖ Ask your vet for local vaccination program (such as the one presented below for those in Northern Region) because disease pattern differs from places to places.
- ❖ Certain vaccines are not advised for laying birds. So consult your vet in all cases.
- ❖ Notes when vaccinating younger chicks (less than 10days old) through drinking water make sure you withdraw water for nothing less than 16 hours to make them thirsty enough. But for those more than 10days old 10-12 hour water starvation is enough depending on where the farm is and the time of the year.

- ☐ Hold the chickens very carefully.

- ☐ Vaccinate the chickens without any strain.

- ☐ Wash the vaccination equipment with hot boiled water or germicide medicine/antiseptic.

- ☐ Do the vaccination program in cold weather condition.

- ☐ Preventive vaccine is always applicable to healthy bird. Never vaccinate an infected bird.

Note that Vaccination program is a must for chicks for keeping them free from all types of diseases. The main advantages of poultry vaccination are listed below.

- ☐ Timely vaccination makes disease resistance power in the body of chick.

- ☐ Help to keep the hen free from infectious poultry diseases.

☐ Disease prevalence will be less.

☐ Mortality rate will reduce.

☐ And low mortality rate = more production = more profit.

There are many types of poultry vaccines are available for layer hens. Marex, Ranikheth, Gumboro, Bruchaities, Bosonto, Foul Pox, Salmonela etc. are used for layer chickens. I will explain more in health management.

I will explain more about health management.

Keeping Growing Chicks

You have to maintain the suggestion listed below for keeping growing layer chickens.

☐ You have to provide the growing chick's special care until they reach 4-5 weeks of age.

☐ After brooding serves them good quality pellet feed. It will make good results in the future. They will produce egg highly. High quality pellet will make the chickens healthy and increase their body weight.

☐ So it is very important to provide them quality pellet feed during growing period.

Egg Production from Commercial Layer Farm

Egg production from a commercial layer farm depends on the care and farm management. If you take good care of your birds and manage them properly, then the production and profit will be high.

☐ Within the first 20 weeks of age, about 5% of hens start laying eggs.

☐ About 10% birds start laying at their 21 weeks of age.

☐ When they reach 26 to 30 weeks of age, they produce highly. Although, it may be different depending on their strain.

☐ After laying a maximum number of eggs, they usually stop laying for a few days.

☐ And after this period, their egg production might reduce slowly.

☐ Egg laying rate and size of eggs increases gradually.

☐   The hens grow till their 40 weeks of age.

☐   Weight and size of eggs increases till their 50 weeks of age.

Method and Importance of Lip Cutting called Debeaking

Debeaking is the removal of the excess outgrowth of the beaks of birds, most especially cockerels and layers long beaks tend to encourage cracking and eating of eggs, pecking on other birds and excessive plucking of feathers. Don't wait for them to peek before you debeak. You may lose some. Debeak your birds as from 6-8 weeks of Age.

Cutting the lip of laying hens is very important. The main benefits are listed below.

☐   Lip cutting help to reduce mutual fights.

☐ It helps to prevent food waste.

☐ You have to cut your chick's lip at their age of on time.

☐ Cut the lip of growing chicken at their 6 to 10 weeks of age.

☐ Cut the lip of chicks 0.2 cm from their nose.

☐ Cut 0.45 cm in case of growing chickens.

☐ Cut the both upper and lower lips.

☐ Don't cut the both lip together. Cut one after another.

☐ Use block chick trimming machine to cut the lips.

Don't cut their lip two days after or before vaccination, after or before using some medicines like sulfur. Don't cut the lip if the hen is in a strain and during adverse weather conditions and if the hen starts laying eggs.

Serve the chicken water mixed with vitamin "K" three days before cutting lips. Wash the lip cutting instrument with antiseptic. Test the edge and temperature of blade. You have to be careful, and don't damage their eyes and tongue. Choose cold weather for cutting their lips. Lip cutting process should be observed by an experienced technician. After cutting lips, serve them water in a deep pot. Provide them some extra energy enriched feed.

Feeding

There are many companies available In Nigeria and other countries of the world which are producing commercial feed for layer chickens. You can buy feed from your local market or make the feed at your own house. You have to be sure that the feed you bought are enriched with essential food value. Protein and mineral are very important for laying hens.

☐ Provide 2% of calcium for two weeks after their birth.

☐ If you notice they are not gaining expected weight, then you have to serve starter feed for eight weeks.

☐ Serve feed two or three times in a day till their 18 weeks of age.

☐ Demand of feed increase very fast when the birds start laying.

☐　　Serve them layer poultry feed according to their age and weights.

☐　　Don't decrease the amount of feed while laying (even if their weight increase).

I will explain more about feeding later.

Water Management

Chickens health depends on the supply of pure, clean and fresh drinking water. You have to provide adequate water according to the demand of your laying hens. For purifying the water, mix 0.3g bleaching per liter. Determine a suitable place to keep the water pot inside the poultry house. Supply cold water during summer season and hot weather, and slightly hot water in cold weather or winter season.

In accordance with the age and species of chickens, food providing can control the weights of chicken. Use sufficient calcium, phosphorus, vitamins, amino acid and other mineral substance in their food. For purifying, water use bleaching powder or chlorine. If you follow the methods mentioned above, then you can make better profit from your layer poultry farming business.

Case study: Testimony of battery cage system

After an extensive reading of books and research on the internet, the beleaguered farmer learnt of the caging system which is preferred because it is hygienic, comfortable and safe to birds. It is also efficient as it is cheaper and takes a high number of birds in a little space.

He says the management of cages was much easier than the deep litter system, which he says exposes chicken to disease. Instead of using water troughs that can be unhygienic, water is supplied by automatic pumps that only allow water to trickle down when pecked by chickens. "I can easily account for every chicken and know which one is laying eggs so that those that have stopped laying are sold off," he said.

High standards of hygiene are maintained at the farm. The gates are locked and visitors have to disinfect their feet before entering the poultry grounds while the houses are disinfected every month.

Chicken are vaccinated from when they are young and therefore are free from many diseases According to David Rotich, an animal health technician and artificial insemination expert for Parksons Agrovet in Kericho, the deep litter system is unsuitable because it exposes birds to itchiness that de-feathers them and coccidiosis that causes diarhoea.

De-feathering, he explained, is as a result of small mites that hide in the dusty floors of the deep litter systems and feed on chicken at night.

"The chicken will scratch and end up losing feathers. But the worst is coccidiosis, where waste comes out with blood stains. It affects the feeding system of chicken and lowers the production of eggs," Rotich said.

He said cages also reduce cannibalism and increase productivity. You choose to keep Rhode Island breed because they lay eggs longer and do not grow old early.

"With the kind of set up in cages, we don't need a lot of staff.

"With my half-acre, I would have kept a maximum of 2,000 chickens. Now I have four times that in the same space.

Sophie Miyumo, a poultry scientist with a smallholder indigenous chicken improvement programme, says the cage system is economical because some cubes extend upwards, allowing more room for birds. "It is recommended that the deep litter system takes up four to six birds per metre square whereas in caging, each cube takes up a maximum of four birds, providing floor area of 450 to 525 square centimeters per bird. This makes it ideal for urban areas where land is scarce. " says Sophie.

The Egerton University lecturers, however, advise that caging is more suitable for layers, and not broilers or indigenous chicken which tend to grow too big for the cubicles in the cages.

Chapter 6

Indigenous breed Hens

Indigenous breed chicken is an existing resource in a number of households in Nigeria and other African countries like Kenya, South Africa etc. It is very rare coming across a home that does not have an average of 5 Indigenous breed or indigenous chicken for family subsistence. It is also common to have each of the family members owning chicken in the home from the heads of the household to young primary school children who are ordinarily given a hen to 'try their luck' in Indigenous breed chicken farming in Nigeria and thus address their own private needs like school books and pencils when their chicken multiply.

It is also a source of eggs and ready cheap source of protein meat for 'change of diet in settings of poverty. Finally it is a source of almost ready income in cases of emergencies like purchase of drugs to address family illness, buy soap for cleaning among other small but equally important household needs or requirements.

Smallholder poultry production is therefore a very powerful tool to easily generate income because farmers are basically not re-inventing the wheel but basically working smart on what they have been doing for generations. If we are focused on getting people to take the first steps towards earning significant money from farming, communities that have a history of indigenous breed chicken rearing have to be mobilized through small investments in indigenous chicken production. Smallholder poultry keeping has the potential to change people's way of life because it offers the farmers a number of advantages:

Flexible Production:

This kind of production system at the village level can be adapted or done in different agro-ecological areas thus not limiting in its scope of generating income and particularly the remote and poorer neighborhoods that are resource constrained. The local population only needs to increase their production with only very minimal inputs. This kind of flexibility ensures that anybody almost anywhere in Nigeria and indeed in West and East Africa can keep indigenous breed chicken.

Low labour Requirements:

Indigenous breed chickens in the remote villages are given only what food leftovers are available but largely left to roam and scavenge for their own food. Direct labour going into their rearing is very minimal making it one of the easiest undertakings for low-income earners.

Inexpensive Housing and Low Input:

Indigenous breed chicken can be kept in any housing that is made using locally available resources and therefore does not require huge investments in housing construction. They are hardy and can live in any condition provided they are not visited by extremes of temperature.

Income Generation:

Indigenous breed chicken farming can earn any family enough income to help them respond to their basic needs through personal selling by the locals in local markets, to neighbours, institutions like schools, hospitals and in community social events like funerals and weddings.

Indigenous breed chicken farming may also be the first rung on the livestock ladder that allows smallholder farmers to progress through increase of economic activities to improve their circumstances. A farmer may keep chicken, save and buy a goat or sheep which multiplies and are sold to buy a cow that supplies milk for the family and earns income.

Indigenous breed chicken farming can therefore be employed successfully among the smallholder farmers in rural and semi-urban settings to generate income if farmers are adequately assisted with basic capacity building in increasing production, strengthening financial access and linkages and access to markets so that farmers can make contract sales and plan with their lives.

We also need to employ effective gender-sensitive methodologies to ensure the organized and profitable rearing of poultry is a source of improved livelihoods not pain in these struggling households where sometimes the chicken belong to the wife during production but ownership cedes to the man at point of sale and use of the money so realized.

Indigenous breed hens such as Rainbrow Rooster, Kenbro or Noiler chickens can be reared both for eggs and meat. These chicken needed to be fed for five to six months before they will start laying eggs, though they don`t lay as much eggs as layers. Some of them that are reared for meat as well take much longer time to mature than broilers.

For many years, poultry farmers in Nigeria and other African countries have been rearing exotic breeds for commercial purposes.

The birds, which lay hundreds of eggs annually, have been the darling of many farmers. But time seems to be up for the exotic breeds that include Leghorn as Nigerian farmers embrace indigenous chicken that is hardy and offers better returns.

The indigenous hens have taken the poultry industry by storm, with thousands of farmers ditching the exotic breeds for the new one. Many farmers rush to buy new indigenous chicken breeds coming into the market without knowing their qualities only to end up with regrets and losses. Poultry keeping is now one of the most popular agribusiness enterprises that many people in Nigeria want to go into.

However, many farmers rush into it without the most basic information on how they can do it the right way. The quail fiasco two years ago no doubt left many farmers with empty pockets when they made huge investments in quail rearing leading to glut in the market and a fall in prices. Many farmers do not seem to have learnt a lesson.

Currently, there are a lot of rumours, and misguided exaggerations about new chicken breeds that are said to do much better than local indigenous breeds in production, enticing farmers to spend a lot of their money in search of the breeds which they only learnt about in newspaper articles and adverts.

In this issue, I would like to shed light on the breeds available in the country and their qualities so that farmers can make informed decisions on the best type of breed they can keep to get good returns by making the best choice from the various breeds in the market.

Kenbro chicken

The Kenbro breed is a dual-purpose (meant for eggs and meat production) breed which was specifically developed to serve the western Nigeria market that has a high demand for chickens. It was introduced into the country about a decade ago by Kenchic

Ltd to meet the demand for farmers who would prefer a breed that requires less intensive management than hybrid chickens.

Kenbro is more resistant to diseases compared to hybrid birds. It can survive on free range. The bird matures faster with proper feeding and starts laying eggs at 5 months. It can attain up to 4kg with proper feeding. Kenchic produces more than 20,000 birds from this breed in a week but some farmers breed the birds and sell to others.

The quality of birds produced by such farmers is low because it is only the company that has the parent stock that can produce high quality birds. Kenbro is a heavy feeder and this is one reason it is able to put more weight than other indigenous chickens.

Noiler chicken

The Noiler is similar breed to Kuroiler and a dual-purpose breed that was introduced and developed in Nigeria by AMO Farm Sieberer Hatchery, popularly known as Amo Hatchery. They are hybrid product of broiler and cockerels conditions like cockerels and are able to withstand most common diseases of poultry chickens and are very resistant to adverse climate. Hence they develop a lot of meat like broiler Like Kenbro, Noiler can survive on free range, but they need to feed continuously, a reason why they put on weight faster than do indigenous chickens; at 4 months Noiler chickens can weigh up to 3kg and 4kg in 6 months.

Farmers rearing this breed say it has tastier meat compared to indigenous chickens; their meat is also soft and tender. Its eggs are larger than those of indigenous chickens. A Noiler hen can lay between 140-150 eggs in a year. However, Noiler's quality goes down when they are crossed with indigenous chickens.

Farmers keeping them say Noiler birds are scavengers that can live on household food leftovers and related agricultural waste. Like local indigenous chickens, Noiler chickens are resistant to most diseases although farmers are advised to vaccinate them in the same way they do other chickens.

However, one big disadvantage with Noiler chickens is that the hens cannot sit on their eggs to hatch. Many farmers discover this fact too late. Noiler chickens are therefore suitable only for farmers with incubators.

Small- scale farmers in the rural areas who rely on hens to hatch chicks can only order fresh stock of chicks every time they want new stock for breeding. Indeed poultry farmers in rural areas in Nigeria are already raising questions on the sustainability of this breed among resource poor communities who cannot manage to buy new stocks every time they want to rear new batches of birds.

Farmers interested in Noiler day-old chicks can contact Leonard Charles on 08065467828.

Rainbow Rooster chicken

Like the Noiler breed, Rainbow Rooster is dual purpose breed meaning that farmers can keep it for both meat and eggs, multi-coloured dual purpose, low input bird which can be put on free range. However, it is a heavy feeder, which is able to put on weight fast attaining 3kg to 4kg in 6 months. However, like the Noiler breed, the Rainbow Rooster hen cannot sit on the eggs to hatch; so farmers who want to keep this breed must have an incubator for hatching.

The breed is therefore not suitable for small-scale farmers in the rural areas who cannot be able to buy incubators mainly for lack of electricity supply.

The indigenous birds are the way to go for any farmer in search of better returns.

The fact that they are similar to the local breeds kept by millions of families make them more appealing. Indigenous breed chickens are the best thing to have happened to Nigerian poultry farmers, who are faced with high cost of feeds. A 50kg bag of chick, layers or broilers mash is being sold at an average of N3, 500. The birds are best-suited for local conditions, require no special feeds, are dual-purpose and their meat is sweet because they exercise.

They are easy to establish for low-income farmers because they are kept under semi-intensive system," he said. He noted that with Indigenous breed birds, farmers who have incubators can hatch their own eggs. A tray of fertilized eggs is currently being sold at N1, 000, which gives farmers more income. According to Nigeria Poultry Farmers Association, there are 32 million chickens in the Nigeria as a nation, six million of which are commercial hybrids.

The higher returns of Kari 'Indigenous breed' chicken

For many years, poultry farmers in Nigeria have been rearing exotic breeds for commercial purposes. The birds, which lay hundreds of eggs annually, have been the darling of many farmers. But time seems to be up for the exotic breeds that include Leghorn as Nigerian farmers embrace indigenous chicken that is hardy and offers better returns.

Cockerel

Cockerel poultry farming is one of the lucrative farming enterprises in most countries in Agriculture sector. Poultry meat mainly comes from two sources: broilers and cockerel. The small poultry farmer prefers to rear cockerel than broiler because of low cost and lesser susceptibility to disease compared to broiler production. Cockerels are raised in both urban and rural areas. Cockerel is a male chicken under one year of age.

Benefit of Cockerel production or farming;

The meat is tasty and well-accepted; there is no taboo against eating of the meat.

- ❖ It can be raised on small and large-scale.
- ❖ Cockerel is hardy and less susceptible to disease compared to other poultry.
- ❖ It can be raised under intensive and semi-intensive system of production.
- ❖ The meat is low in fat and cholesterol compared to broiler's meat.
- ❖ It is commonly raised by local people.
- ❖ It is a good source of animal protein and it is of high biological value.
- ❖ It is a good source of income to farmers. The business can be combined with other farm business.
- ❖ The day old cockerel could be easily sourced.
- ❖ Cockerel marketing is all year round and not seasonal.
- ❖ At maturity it can reach market weight of 3-4kg.

There are different types of cockerel breeds in the world. The breeds could be classified as; (i) Local cockerel (ii) Exotic cockerel.

Chapter 7

Selecting Your Farm location

Selecting a good farm location for your poultry business is very important. You should select such a location which has all required facilities and favorable for your business. It can be slightly far from the town, where land and labor is pretty cheap. But don't setup the farm too far from the town because most of the towns have high density population, and you have to target that market. Also try to avoid setting up the farm in residential areas, because poultry farms produce offensive odor. While selecting the farm location, consider transportation system and medication facilities also.

There are few factors that make location a very important issue to be considered when thinking about poultry business and here they are;

❖ Your market. Since what you want to sell is chickens and eggs a location near city and towns is usually good. Why not city or town itself?

❖ Odour and noise. Who can live near a big poultry farm? In fact, it's against the law in many places to have your bird's farm near houses. Also consider:

❖ Cost of land. As I have said earlier, the cost of land in some cities could be enough for starting and running a poultry farm in some nearby towns

❖ Consider the above points to decide where you will locate your farm.

In almost any country in the world that you visit, you would find a huge market for poultry products because poultry products are regarded as healthy meals. Eggs for instance, are recommended to be eaten everyday as a source of protein.

The profitability of poultry business is not a subject for debate because it is already established that poultry farming is profitable. Whether you would make profits or not depends on how you run the business.

One of the major determinants of profitability in poultry farming is site selection. You have to select a very good location for your poultry farm in order to succeed. Below are important factors to consider when selecting a site for your poultry farm-:

1. Neighborhood

Nobody likes noise and strong offensive odors close to their homes. One of the ways to quickly run into problems with environmental protection agencies is to site your poultry farm close to a living area. Of course, you can start your little backyard poultry farm in your home and as long as you keep it clean and make use of noise prevention techniques, you won't have challenges but once you decide to go commercial, it is better to look for a farm land to site your poultry. Farm lands are usually out of town and the only neighbors you would have are other farmers who wouldn't be bothered with the noise or smell coming from your own farm.

2. Setbacks

One other important factor to consider is the setbacks to provide in order to prevent water quality problems and nuisance. There are recommended guidelines for setbacks. For instance, it is recommended that you provide a setback of at least 500 feet from other residences that are not poultry farms; for public areas and places like schools or churches, the recommended setback is 1,500 feet, for public roadways 150 feet and for streams, 100 feet. A visit to the local town planning office would further open your eyes to the rules and guidelines to follow for setback provision.

3. Utilities and public amenities

You would need some public utilities like electricity and water to run your commercial poultry farm. Therefore, you have to consider the availability of these facilities in the area where you have chosen to site your poultry farm. If these facilities are not readily available, *what would be the cost of providing alternative source power*?

If you are setting up your poultry farm in a place where constant electricity supply is a fairytale, you have to look at the area and find out how regularly they get electricity and how much it would cost you to buy a generator and fuel it monthly. This is very important because unplanned electricity costs can cripple your business by seizing too much of your profits.

4. Road Network

Next, you must consider the road network in the place where you plan to site your poultry farm. You would need to have access to very good roads to ease the supply process. Customers can get discouraged from buying from you if the road to your farm is too bad. Make sure you choose a place that is accessible and has very good roads.

5. Expansion Plan

Your business is definitely going to grow. Just manage it efficiently and you will see. Hence, you need to start planning for the growth of your business; you must ensure that the site you choose has enough space for expansion. For instance, if you start with 1,500 birds, soon enough your herd would grow to about 3,000 birds and you cannot rear 3,000 birds in the same space you used for 1500 birds.

Therefore, it is very important to plan adequately for expansion in this business. You may even want to delve into other aspects of poultry farming in the future and you need space to be able to do that. The same thing also applies if you want to add poultry feed production to your line of business. You don't have to start looking for space each time you consider a new business plan when you have already made plans for space before you started out.

6. Topography

The topography of the area is also important. You have to consider how leveled the site is because if it is not properly leveled, you would need to spend a lot of money on grading to be able to get a well leveled ground for construction and that would shoot up construction costs.

7. Drainage

Ensure that the site has proper drainage system. Absence of a good drainage system may lead to erosion and cause great problems for your farm. You should also take the slope of the area into consideration; ensure that water would flow out of the place and not into the buildings.

8. Wind direction

The prevailing wind direction of the area would give you an idea of how much distance you need to provide between your poultry farm and other residences. Like I already mentioned, odor is a great problem in poultry farming and if you don't want your neighbors complaining and reporting you to the authorities you must take steps to reduce the effect of odors on your neighbor's residence and then use distance as a cushioning strategy.

9. Waste Management

Another factor to consider is waste management. Some of the waste from your chickens can be used as manure but you need enough space to collect and process it.

10. Natural Disasters

You should also find out about the area and natural disasters. You must know what natural disasters like landslides, floods or sand storms the area is prone to and what preventive measures to take to reduce the effects if and when they happen.

FACTORS TO CONSIDER WHEN BUYING POULTRY FARMS FOR SALE

Layers Poultry farming is a very lucrative but highly technical business, people who are going into poultry farming as new comers need a lot of technical know-how to be able to start and manage a poultry farming business. Buying a poultry farm from an already established farmer who now wishes to sell his farm off gives you some leverage. You can save upon a lot of costs when you buy a poultry farm instead of building one from the scratch.

However, you have to be careful when buying a poultry farm for sale. Some of the important things you have to consider are-:

1. Location of the farm

You have to consider management of the farm when you want to make your purchase. Poultry farming is a business that needs lot of attention and monitoring, the birds have to be fed, eggs have to be picked and the birds must have access to clean water for drinking. All this may not be easy to do if the farm is too far away from your home. The farm must be close to where you live if you want to manage it yourself or have living quarters for whoever would be employed to manage it.

2. Proximity to market

You also need to consider the nearness to customers. You would most likely be selling eggs which are best delivered fresh and that is just one of the reasons why you should choose a farm that is close enough to your target market. You also need to consider the costs of transporting your products from the farm to your customers. It's not cost effective for your farm to be too far from your customers because the costs of transportation would gulp down too much of your profit.

3. Construction of chicken house

A well-constructed chicken house increases productivity. The sizes and the specifications are very important. A lot of poultry farmers engage the services of expert to advise and assist them in construction of a standard chicken house. If you are buying a poultry farm, you may not have control over the way it would be constructed but you must ensure that it is well constructed.

There are two major types of poultry houses; the deep litter system or the battery cage. The deep litter system involves placing the birds on a floor which is already covered in saw dust. The saw dust makes it easier for chicken waste to be managed. To clean the chicken house, all you have to do is to cover the floor with another layer of sawdust or remove one layer and spread another layer of sawdust. As for the battery cage system, the chickens are kept in a cage high off the ground so that their waste can drop to the floor for disposal.

Each method has its own unique advantages and disadvantages so, before you buy a poultry farm, it is advisable to seek the advice of experts on how suitable the method of construction used for the chicken house in the poultry farm you are about to buy would be for you.

4. Source of water supply

You must also ensure that the poultry farm you are about to buy has regular access to clean water. The farm must at least have a well, a tap or a functioning borehole. This is because regular access to clean drinking water is very important for the survival of poultry birds. Dehydration is one of the fastest killers of chicken and if the farm doesn't have a reliable source of water supply, you may be forced to start buying water which would be stressful and expensive for you at the end of the day.

5. Zoning laws

You must also check for the zoning laws and regulations of the area where the poultry farm is located. For all you know the owner might just be selling because of zoning problems. Therefore, you should conduct a proper investigation into the zoning requirements of that area to be on the safe side.

6. Costs

As for the costs, there are factors to be considered. First, you must know the value of lands in the area and compare with the amount the owner is asking for. You may engage the services of estate valuation experts to carry out a valuation for you. You should also consider the costs of repairs and remodeling. If the costs of reconstruction plus the cost of purchase would be close to the cost of building your own farm from the scratch at the end of the day, then the latter may be a smarter option.

7. Security

You have to consider the level of security of the farm. Most poultry farm site their farms in rural areas very far from civilization because lands in these areas are cheaper but the problem is that these places sometimes have lower level of security. If your poultry farm is located in a bush far away from civilization, there are chances of robbery, thefts and even threats to life. Pests and wild animals are also threats to the security of your poultry farm. So, you should ensure the area is free from pets, wild animals and any other type of security threats.

8. Space

A poultry farm must be big enough to accommodate growth and expansion in the future. Space also promotes ventilation which reduces disease outbreaks and increase production in poultry birds. You would also need a lot of space for storage and sorting. Therefore, you have to consider the space factor when buying a poultry farm as well.

9. Hatchery

A poultry farm that has its own hatchery is a plus for every poultry farmer. When you have your own hatchery, you won't have to take your eggs to another place where you would pay for them to be hatched or have to buy day old chicks. This gives you access to chicks and helps your business to grow faster.

10. Storage

Lastly, you should go for a poultry farm that has its own storage space. When you collect your eggs, you would need a place keep them before you supply to your customers. This is why you need a poultry farm with a storage space.

These factors would guide you in making a decision to make the right choice when buying a poultry farm. However, if you are new into poultry farming, you should consider hiring

a consultant who is well into the business to guide you and help you make a selection. This can save you a whole lot of money and stress at the end of the day.

WHAT IS THE BEST POULTRY FENCING OPTION

Predators are one of the major challenges poultry owners' faces and that is why it is necessary to buy into considering an effective fencing option when designing your poultry farm. If predators find their way into your poultry; they are likely going to keep coming until they eat up all the available birds in your poultry.

Consequently, if you are into poultry farming, much more than thinking of ways to expand your market, you should also make provision for ways to protect your birds from predators such as snakes, badgers, e.t.c. As a matter of fact, your interest should be on how to install an effective poultry fencing system that can give you the guarantee that come rain or sun shine, the birds in your poultry will be well protected.

The major poultry fencing option available are Chicken Wire which is also known as rabbit wire in the marketplace and Chicken Netting. The choice you make on the best poultry fencing option that you want to use in your poultry farm will be largely dependent are some factors.

Some the factors to consider before choosing the right poultry fencing option are the kind of predators your birds will be exposed to, climatic condition of the location you intend building your poultry farm and also the geographical composition of your choice location.

Having stated some of the factors that can influence your choice of fencing option now let me examine the two major options available:

1. Chicken Wire (Rabbit Wire)

If you are conversant with poultry farms, you will realize that most of them make use of chicken wire for fencing their poultry. Chicken wire happens to be stronger and a better option when you are protecting against predators like snakes and badgers, etc.

For ages, wild cats and badgers are the major predators that poultry farmers in Nigeria are contending with. This wire is always on top of their games when it comes to preventing these predators from eating up their birds.

The fact that badgers can scale fences that are as high as 5 ft makes it even more necessary to build your fence to be as high as 6 ft and also ensure that you bury the fence up to 6 inches or more in the soil. This is necessary because badgers are known to dig the ground to make way for easy passage. They pass underneath the ground to enter the poultry.

It is also very important to ensure that you make use of solid wood to run through the base of your chicken wire fence so that it will make it strong enough when subjected to pressure.

2. Chicken Netting

Another option for poultry fencing is chicken netting. This option is highly suitable in locations where the poultry farmers don't get to contend with predators such as badgers. Chicken netting is not as strong as chicken wire (rabbit wire) and most poultry farmers make use of it when their major intention is to keep their birds from straying away from the parameter designed for them.

As a matter of fact, Chicken Netting is basically what is needed when the birds you have in your poultry are likely going to fly away if they have the opportunity. It is cheaper to construct and install chicken netting as against chicken wire (rabbit wire) fencing.

Whatever decision you make, just make sure that you design poultry fences in such a way that it may be easier for you to access your poultry. You would have to create an entrance (a door) and ensure that the door is well secured enough to prevent predators from breaking into your poultry.

In essence, the best poultry fencing option for you is solely dependent on the challenges that you are likely going to face in the location you choose to build your own poultry. That is why it is important to conduct your feasibility studies and also ask loads of questions from poultry owners around you.

Factors to Consider When Fencing Your Poultry Farm

If you are looking towards starting your own poultry farm business, then you must ensure that you consider some key factors when designing and building a fence for your poultry farm. The truth is that if you do not get it right with your poultry fencing, you stand the chance of running at a loss in your poultry business because you would likely lose your birds to predators and flu.

Building a proper fencing for your poultry farm will help you maximize profits in your poultry business because you will be able to take care of predators that are likely to eat up your birds, you will be able to ensure proper ventilation and also to prevent excessive wind from getting to your birds. Proper fencing system will prevent intruders from getting to your poultry, it will help you restrict the movement of your birds to only the perimeters where you want them to be.

So if you are drawing your plan for your poultry farm business, you should ensure that you also consider building proper fencing as well. *Now let us quickly consider the factors to consider when fencing your poultry farm;*

a. The Climatic Condition of the Environment Where Your Poultry Is Located

The Climatic condition of the environment you intend building your poultry farm is one of the factors that you need to consider when fencing your poultry farm. If the location you choose to start your poultry farm is prone to hurricane, cyclone or tornadoes, then you must build a very strong fence that can withstand such strong wind. Besides the climatic condition of the area has a great effect in the productivity of your poultry business.

b. The Kind of Birds You Have In Your Poultry

The kind of birds you intend raising in your poultry farm is a key factor that will determine your fencing option. For example, if your intention of starting your poultry business is to layers, broilers or indigenous breed hens along side with birds like quails that can fly, then you should consider fencing not just the perimeter of the poultry, but also you can cover the top with chicken to prevent the birds from flying away.

c. The Type of Predators Your Birds / Fowls Be Exposed To

The type of predators your birds / fowls are likely going to be exposed to should inform your fencing choice. If your poultry will be exposed to predators such as badgers or snakes, then you should choose a fence built with rabbit wire and planks. The rabbit wire should be buried in the ground to prevent the predators from digging their way into your poultry.

d. Easy Accessibility

When making a choice for the design of your poultry farm fencing, you should consider easy accessibility of workers and customers. If your poultry farm is designed in such a way that customers can come in to purchase birds and eggs, then you should design your fencing in such a way that people can easily access it; you would be required to construct more than one gate / door to facilitate easy entry and exit especially if you have high human traffic in your poultry farm.

e. Effective Security System

When designing a fence for your poultry farm, you should consider effective security system. If possible you can put alarms at strategic points around your poultry farm fence. This alarm can be triggered whenever someone tries to break into your poultry.

CCTV can be installed in strategic places around your poultry farm to help you effectively monitor your poultry farm.

f. Easy Ventilation

Another important factor that you should consider when building your poultry farm fence is easy ventilation for your birds. If there is no proper ventilation for your poultry because of your choice of fencing materials, you are likely going to lose some of your birds to bird flu that can easily spread when there is poor ventilation. So ensure that you put in place proper ventilation when considering your fencing option for your poultry farm.

g. Construction Cost and Your Budget

Construction cost and your budget is another factor you need to consider if you want to build fence for your poultry farm. Of course you cannot afford to spend beyond your financial capacity, that is why you should look at all the fencing options you have and then choice the one that is economical and that can easily fit into your budget. The bottom line is that it should serve the purpose for which it was built for.

h. Environmental Hazard

The environmental hazard your birds / fowls are likely going to be exposed to should inform your poultry farm fencing option. You can make enquiries from the environmental safety department in Nigeria to ensure that you get the required information that will guide you when designing a fence for your poultry farm.

i. Safety for Both Birds and Human

When making plans to design and build fence for your poultry farm, safety for both birds and human should top the list of the factors you must consider before going ahead to construct a fence for your poultry farm. Just ensure that the type of material to be used for your poultry farm fencing is strong enough to withstand pressure so that it will not collapse.

j. The Size of Your Poultry Farm

The size of your poultry farm is another factor to consider when designing the fence for your poultry farm. If your poultry farm covers a large portion of land area, then you must build a fencing system that will have security post at strategic points. You can as well install CCTV to help you with effective monitoring of your poultry farm. But if your poultry farm is small, then there would be no need to install security post all around the fence; it can easily be managed.

There you have it; the 10 factors to consider when fencing your poultry farm.

Chapter 8

Equipment and Appliances you will need

One of the keys to a successful poultry business is getting the right equipment. Therefore, before you start your hen poultry farm, you must do proper equipment planning. Some of the crucial factors to consider when buying poultry equipment for your farm include-:

1. Age of Birds-:

Every age of your birds is unique in their needs. The type of equipment you would use to rear chicks birds is different from those of chickens. Each life stage of your flock has its own unique method of rearing it.

Chicks will need warmth during their young growing stage but once they are big enough they will no longer need it. Therefore you will be budgeting for your flock's equipments as need arise at each life stage.

2. Space-:

This is another very important factor to consider when buying poultry equipment is the size of your poultry farm. Some poultry tools and equipment are quite small and space is not really a challenge, but other equipment is really big and can take up a whole lot of space. You must be able to determine how much space you have for keeping equipment before you buy them. Look at the product information for dimensions and specifications and then determine if you have enough space for the equipment.

3. Price Comparison-:

Yet another important thing to take note of is the price. There are lots of things to be bought and saving a couple of shillings on some items is not a bad idea. The best places to compare price of equipment is online e.g. olx.com and Jiji.com, etc.

You would find a lot of equipment from manufacturers online and once you have looked into their product catalogue and made certain that they have what you want, call them up for negotiations but be wiser when it comes to online payment.

You don't have to buy equipment at the prices stated on their website or page especially if you are just buying in bulk. You can always negotiate and you would be surprised that most suppliers would be willing to offer you further price reductions and discounts if you ask for it.

4. Custom-made or Ready-Made-:

What a lot of commercial poultry farmers do is to decide on their needs, draw up some designs and specifications to fulfill their needs and then forward the designs to poultry equipment manufacturers like Lenarc-phil technologies Nig. Ltd. workers to custom-make the designs to meet with your specifications.

The Feeder

You can adopt this method too and use local welders and equipment manufacturers around you but if you feel that it would be too much stress; then you should opt for ready-made poultry equipment with pre-determined designs and specifications.

5. Technical Know-How-:

You must also consider who and how it would be operated. If you are buying incubation and hatching equipment for instance; you must know how to use it or at least have someone who can operate it for you. You should also consider buying equipment with manuals that would carefully explain how it should be assembled and used.

Some poultry equipment is relatively easy to use while some require a learning curve process. Ensure that the company you are buying from is ready to provide support during the period which you are learning how to use the equipment in order to avoid serious mistakes that can lead to losses.

6. Cleaning-:

This is especially important when constructing your poultry housing system. You must consider how waste like poop and chicken droppings or waste feed would be cleaned. This may seem like something that is very easy but practically, it is not. You have to keep the poultry clean in order to keep the birds in good health and keep the farm free from diseases.

But chicken droppings come almost every minute and it's really hard to keep a poultry farm clean without mechanical assistance. It is therefore important for you to go with the construction pattern with optimal waste management system especially if you don't have many laborers to help out.

7. Cash flow-:

Cash flow is yet another important factor to consider before buying poultry equipment. In the process of managing your poultry farm; you would need constant flow of cash. The birds cannot go hungry or it would affect their growth. They may even start to die. Therefore, you must always ensure that there is enough money to carry on all operational aspects of the business like electricity, heating and ventilation management, payment of workers, feeding and healthcare. What I am saying in essence is that you shouldn't buy equipment at the expense of other aspects of farm operation management.

8. Technology-:

Technology is also very important when buying poultry equipment. As you already know, technology is always evolving and you don't want to be caught using archaic equipment or buying equipment that other tech-savvy farmers are already moving from. Therefore, you must conduct your research carefully to be sure that you are buying the latest poultry equipment.

9. Online or Offline-:

Lastly, you have to decide on whether you want to buy on the internet or from local merchants. Each method has its pros and cons. One major disadvantage of buying online is that you don't get to test what you are buying and you may also have shipping costs added to the costs of product which makes it more expensive to buy online In some cases, Ensure that weigh all the pros and cons before you make your purchase.

What are the poultry equipment you will need?

The nice thing about raising chickens is that you need very little to get started. The majority of the expense is in the coop and run. Most of the other things that chickens require, might be something you already have at home that can be re-purposed.

There are so many products out on the market nowadays that it can be hard to figure out what a newbie layers chicken keeper really needs. Here is a generous list of things you might consider having on hand to make layers chicken keeping a little more convenient. By no means do you need all of this, but for people who have never raised chickens, it is my hope that this list can give you an idea of what the future might hold for you and your flock, and give you some ideas for what your flock might require.

This list breaks down what chickens need at different age levels, and a few other ideas for egg storage, clothing and protection for you. It also lists a few things to keep your coop clean.

Sharing equipment, buying used and cleaning it properly

There are good things and bad things about buying used equipment or sharing poultry equipment. The good things are that you save money, practice recycling and can help out a friend in need and vice versa. The problem is that when you share equipment you could also be sharing potential diseases and parasites.

If you plan to use used equipment with your flock, be sure to sanitize it properly. Remove all dirt by washing in hot soapy water and a good glug of bleach. Get in all crevasses. Use steel wool or sandpaper on metal objects. Especially around rusted areas that might hold bacteria in the pitted crevasses. Dry objects in the sun for additional sanitation.

Hatching

If you plan to hatch out your first chicks, you're in for a real treat! There are few things more amazing to witness. But you'll need some equipment to get you started.

Incubator:

There are several incubator designs on the market, and you can even make your own. My experience has been that you get what you pay for. I've purchased the inexpensive Styrofoam models and have had little success. Our Incubator of choice is the Brinsea Mini Advanced. It is truly foolproof and is great for first time hatchings.

Lenarc-phil Technologies Limited - **08152838211** sells highly advanced automatic eggs incubators in Nigeria and in East Africa. They also give free training services to farmers regarding various kinds of poultry keeping and at the same time provide a wide market for their customer's products.

60 Eggs Incubator (Price = N90, 000)

☐   Can hatch 60 chicken egg

☐   Highly efficient with High Hatch rate

☐   Uses advanced digital controls for automatic temperature regulation.

☐   Has low power consumption of below 80w.

☐   Portable and easy to carry.

Neochicks 60 eggs incubator

- **48 chicken Eggs incubator (Price = N80, 000)**

- It is fully automatic and can hold 48 chicken eggs.

- It uses highly advanced digital controls and is very precise.

- High Hatch rate

48 Eggs automatic Incubator

☐   High Hatch rate

☐   Can use a solar or a battery directly.

☐   Can also use the electricity.

☐   It is fully automatic and can hold 48 chicken eggs.

☐   It uses highly advanced digital controls and is very
precise.

48 Eggs Solar Incubator

1232 Eggs Incubator

☐   Free generator for back up purposes in case of power blackout.

☐   Fully Automatic, (humidity control, temperature control, turning, ventilation)

☐   High Hatching efficiency

☐   1 Year Warranty

☐   Automatic water refill system

- ☐   long life span of over 20 years

2112 Eggs Incubator

- ☐   Free generator for back up purposes in case of power blackout.

- ☐   Fully Automatic (humidity control, temperature control, turning, ventilation)

- ☐   High hatching efficiency

- ☐   2 Year Warranty

☐   Automatic water refilling system

☐   Long life span.

☐   Free maintenance and servicing

4928 Eggs Incubator

☐ Free generator for back up purposes in case of power blackout.

☐ Fully Automatic, (humidity control, temperature control, turning, ventilation)

☐ High hatch rate

☐ Low power consumption (Solar Compatible)

☐ 1 Year Warranty

☐ Automatic water refill system

☐ long life span of over 20 years

☐ Vaccines, vitamins and minerals for various types of poultry birds

Let's move to the next equipment you will need.

Candler

Candling your eggs allows you to see which eggs are progressing and which might be dead or infertile. It is recommended that you remove any eggs that are not going to hatch from your incubator. Dead eggs when kept in moist warm incubator temperatures can spoil and sometimes explode spreading rotted material on your vital eggs and likely infect other good eggs.

Candling can be as simple as using a flashlight in a dark closet,

Or to make things easier I recommend the OvaScope Egg Scope.

Brooder

Once your chicks hatch or once you buy day old chicks you will need a place to keep them. A brooder is an area where chicks can be kept warm and safe. You will need:

Container:

A brooder can be anything from a cardboard box to a large Rubbermaid container. It must be large enough to fit growing chicks. It should be water resistant to protect floors and draft free.

Chick drinker

It's important to use a drinker that is designed especially for chicks. This prevents drowning and minimizes water spillage. Water should be changed daily and raised as the chicks get taller to avoid soiling and walking in the water. If you have a lot of chicks buy a size appropriate drinker and keep it out of the brooder heating element.

Feeder:

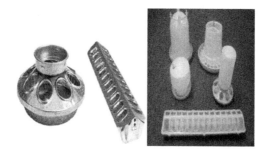

Any dish can be used to feed chicks so long as it's low enough for them to reach. Chicks should be provided with a 20% protein starter feed at all times. The feeders designed for chicks prevent waste because the small access holes limit scratching and spreading the feed. The gravity feed also provides a constant source of food without having to fill the dish several times a day.

Heat lamp or Poultry brooder heater

You will need a heat source to keep your chicks warm. One of the cheapest ways is to provide a heat light bulb and the hood attachment. Red bulbs help reduce picking because chickens are attracted to the color red. If all the light is red, they can't pick one red thing out from another like a scab from a chick mate.

You can also provide a dome heating element like the Chick Brooder, which is very safe, but a little more expensive.

Bedding:

I am in love with pine pellets. They are super absorbent, and the pine oils eliminate odors. They also reduce dust due to scratching. Pine flake bedding and shredded paper bedding are other options.

Cedar bedding is not recommended as it can cause lung and eye irritations.

Grit for chicks: Chicks need grit offered at all times to help them digest their food. Buy grit designed for chicks as the size of the granules will be smaller and prevent choking.

Teenagers

I consider chicks who have feathered out to be teenagers. That time after chick-dom but before adulthood.

Separation Pen:

If you are adding spring chicks to an existing adult flock, chances are you might need a **separation pen.**

This pen will house teenage birds that are too big to be in a brooder, but too young to join the adult flock. Sometimes this transition can be difficult as the new birds establish pecking order. It's a good idea to have a backup space to keep birds separated.

Waterer or Drinkers

Teenagers can be transitioned to an adult drinker. The chance of drowning lessens as birds get older.

Feeder:

They can start sharing the adult feeders at this point so long as they are positioned low enough for pint sized chickens. You might also find it necessary to purchase a larger feeder if this is your first flock, as adult chickens eat more than chicks.

After 6 weeks chicks can be fed a grower feed at 18% crude protein content.

Grit: Teenagers can also start transitioning to the adult size grit when they are about ¾ the size of an adult.

Roosts: If the chicks are feathered out, they should have no problem roosting on adult roosts.

Adult birds

Coop: Adult chickens need a draft free, ventilated, predator proof coop that protects them from the elements. I will teach you more in Chapter 6: Housing Your Layers

Water drinker:

There are about as many drinkers in the market as there are chicken breeds. The reason for this is because chickens scratch and defecate in their drinker. It is an ongoing battle to keep chickens supplied with fresh, clean water.

There are many different types of drinkers including:

1.   **Metal Vacuum types**

2. Nipple water system

3. Plastic drinkers

My favorite type of drinker is a wide, shallow, rubber dish. It's easy to fill, easy to dump out and easy to clean with a sponge.

Another thing to consider is a **heating element** for your drinker if you live in a climate that experiences cold temperatures. Make sure your drinker will work with a heating element so you don't have to purchase two.

Food:

Egg boxes:

Egg boxes can be purchased readymade, or can be constructed at home from new or recycled equipment. Chickens need about 1 egg box for every 3 to 5 birds.

I prefer the use of layers rearing cage system which has drinkers, feeders and egg laying place all in one.

Cleaning Supplies

Cleaning spray:

There are many cleaning sprays out on the market but I find that a combination of white vinegar and Peroxide clean most things well enough. I also use bleach occasionally, depending on the situation.

Wide shovel:

A wide, flat shovel works wonderful for pine chip or pelleted bedding. It also works great for scooping up the last bits of straw if you use that as bedding.

Pitch fork: Works great for cleaning soiled straw bedding.

Hand trowel: For scraping feces off of roosts/egg boxes

Broom: For cleaning the last bits of soiled bedding before laying down a fresh layer.

Keep a special broom for the coop and barn only.

For your own person

Egg basket:

You don't NEED a fancy egg basket; you can carry your eggs in anything from a bucket to your shirt tails. But with all the adorable baskets on the market, it's fun to have one in your stock.

Muck boots:

Boots not only keep your feet dry and clean, but designating a special pair of boots to be worn in your coop alone helps with bio-security and lessens the chance of spreading disease.

Mask:

It's always smart to wear a mask when cleaning your chicken coop. Dried feces can become airborne when shoveling. This is especially important if you have a walk-in coop.

Gloves:

I'm not a glove person... but gloves are a good way to protect your hands while cleaning and handling your chickens. Chickens can scratch your hands and arms with their claws if you try to hold an untamed chicken. Keep gloves especially for chicken use, in the same way you would muck boots.

Empty egg cartons:

Most farmers always recycle their egg carton and use them over and again. They wash the Styrofoam and plastic ones. If you plan on selling your eggs, some areas require that you use new cartons. These can be purchased at your local feed store.

Egg cleaning supplies:

There's always much debate as to how to clean an egg, or if you should clean them at all. Most farmers do wash their eggs and they have had good luck with the Manna Pro Egg wash, or hot water and dawn dish soap with a scrubby sponge. White vinegar works well to remove stubborn stains.s

Pen to mark the date:

A wax pencil or Sharp-y works well for marking the date on egg shells. This ensures that eggs are always fresh.

That's all the main equipments you need in your layers hens rearing business.

If you are planning to start a layers poultry farm, you would need the right equipment at suitable prices. It is unlikely that when you are starting your poultry farm, you would have a truck load of extra funds to throw around. Most likely, you would be on a tight budget because of the long list of things you have to put in place. This is why you must do everything within your means to cut on costs of buying poultry equipment.

The first step to take in cutting costs of poultry equipment is buying from the right source.

There are three options to consider when buying poultry equipment;

☐ **New Equipment**-: This involves buying new ready-made equipment from suppliers or in the open market.

☐ **Fairly Used Equipment**-: You may find poultry farmers who are going out of business, relocating or selling off their poultry equipment as a result of expansion.

☐ **Custom made equipment**-: Another option is to have your own equipment custom-made specifically for you by manufacturers or local welders. The manufacturers would make the equipment to suit your taste, design and needs.

Chapter 9

Purchasing/Hatching Chicks

After setting everything up and having everything ready, purchase quality chicks from trusted breeder in your area or hatch chicks by yourself especially Indigenous breed chick and start caring them.

Let me talk about how to hatch chicks then later in this chapter I will talk about purchasing chicks.

PRODUCTION OF CHICKS

❖ **Production of fertile Eggs**

Only fertile eggs can be used for hatching mature cocks and hens in the ratio of 1:18 can be raised together in a deep litter house. When the cocks mate with the hens, fertile eggs will be produced.

❖ Incubation

This involves keeping fertile eggs warm so that the embryo will develop to produce a young bird. Incubation could either be natural or artificial.

❖ Natural Incubation

Natural incubation involves the hens which incubate their eggs by sitting on them to keep them warm. Domestic chickens and many other birds normally wait until a clutch of about 10-15 eggs have been laid before they start incubating them once the hen has settled on her clutch of eggs in her nesting box, her body warmth incubates the eggs it is called broody hen.

A hen's body temperature is about 39.4°c, but she controls the incubating temperature by leaving the next more frequently when her temperature is high. This warmth stimulates cell division and development of the embryo. A broody hen will turn her eggs every ten minutes or so throughout the incubating period. This turning of eggs prevents the yolk from stocking to the shell which would prevent proper development of the embryo.

❖ Artificial Incubation

For large scale production of chicks, artificial incubations become necessary. There are many kinds of incubators, but basically an incubator is a box-like structure that is heated by oil, electricity, or gas. The eggs are held in trays and one incubator may be able to hold several thousands of eggs at a time.

- The eggs are sorted out to remove broken or damaged or defective
- Ones.
- The sorted eggs are kept in the cold room with low temperature line to control any further embryonic development.
- The eggs should be fumigated and arranged in tray and placed in the incubator.

Optimum Incubation Conditions

- Temperature is usually 37-39^{oc}
- Relative humidity of 50-60% during the first nineteen days and 75% during the last two days to three days to prevent dehydrating the chicks in the Hatcher.
- Ventilation (Air flow) for free movement of oxygen, nitrogen, carbon dioxide and water vapor through the shell is very important for the development of embryo.
- Egg positioning during incubation. Eggs are usually placed in the incubator with the large end facing upward.
- Egg turning, the eggs are turned regularly in the incubator in order to expose all sides to the incubator conditions and prevent the embryo from sticking to the shell.

- Candling: This is the process of identifying and separating the fertile eggs from the non-fertile ones. This is done from 5-7th day. Fertile eggs have spider-like appearance, with cobweb line of blood vessels.

Infertile eggs look dull and morbid, clear with no spider-like lines second candling is done on the 18th day before transferring to the Hatcher.

Hatching

This involves breaking the incubated eggs for the chicks to emerge. When the eggs have remained for 18days in the pre-hatching incubator, they are transferred to the hatching incubator (hatchery) where they remain until 21 days during which the hatch able eggs are hatched. The day old chicks are usually removed from the incubator a few hours after they are hatched.

Post-Hatching Operations in the Hatchery

Activities or operations that are normally carried out after hatching of eggs are: in the hatchery includes:

- Sexing of chicks into male and female.
- Drying of chicks
- Intra-Ocular (i) NDV Vaccinations
- Sorting out abnormal chicks
- (v)   Packing of normal and healthy chicks.

MANAGEMENT OF DAY OLD CHICKS

TO FINISHING OR LAYING PHASE:

Housing of the birds

- An open-sided house with short solid walls builds preferably with mud or cement blocks should be used. Poultry house in the tropics is very simple consider the following while constructing a poultry house.
- Ventilation: Open sided house provides adequate ventilation in locations with high environmental humidity and temperature; empty feed bags can be used to cover open sides during the cold nights of the year. In cold areas 2-3 feet of the house from foundation should be made with blocks or roofing sheets fan could be used in hot weather to help improve ventilation.

Space Requirement

Overcrowding is the major cause of losses in poultry houses due to egg drinking, pecking, disease spread, poor growth and poor productions. Observe the space requirement as started below.

<u>Age</u>	<u>Space</u>
0-6weeks	10-13 birds/square meter
6-22 weeks	6-9 birds/square meter
22-weeks	8 birds/ square meter

Small size breeds need less space than bigger breeds. For laying next, space allow 4 birds to one nest. You may have to make wooden boxes.

Litter Management

The litter should be kept dry at all times. Wet or damp litter encourages diseases outbreak. Wet or damp litter should be replaced with dry material immediately. Wood shavings are the best litter material in this part of the country.

The chicken house should be thoroughly cleared of the older litter, dusted and washed with detergent. After this, it should be disinfected with a strong and reliable disinfectant like izal, Dettol, etc.

- The equipment should be thoroughly washed
- The house should be allowed to dry and air out for at least 7days before putting new chicks into the house.

❖ Mold-free and dry litter materials such as dust free wood shavings should be evenly spread in the 2 days before the arrival of the chicks.

❖ The right type of feeder and waterer should be placed inside the brooding house; brooding unit should be placed inside the house.

❖ The heating unit should be checked to ensure that everything is in order.

- ❖ Water should be provided in the waterer at least one hour before the chicks arrive, feed should also be available.
- ❖ The heating system should be on at least two hours before the chick arrives, or four hours during harmattan.

The vaccination should be booked or in the fridge and you should be aware of the vaccination schedule.

After the Chicks have arrived

- ❖ The chick box should be unloaded quickly, distributed in the house.
- ❖ The chicks should be carefully counted near the source of heat.
- ❖ The weak ones should be resuscitated by dripping their breaks into water or forcing water down their throat.
- ❖ Some of the chick boxes may be opened up and placed on the floor.
- ❖ Clean newspapers may be spread on the floor feed can be spread on it. Plastic materials are not suitable.
- ❖ The filling of the boxes and the rest of the chick boxes should be burnt immediately.
- ❖ In the first few hours the birds should be watched to ensure that they are drinking and eating and the temperature is right for them. The behavour of the chicks should indicate whether they are comfortable or not.

BROODING

Note: The brooding management procedures for pullet chicks of 0-8 weeks and broiler chicks of 0-4 weeks are basically the same.

This is the process of keeping the poultry house warm for brooding chicks continue the chicks in a smaller space and use 200 watts bulbs were electricity is available. Where there is no electricity gas, stove or charcoal pots with blue flames, i.e. low flame. Avoid smoke; else the chicks will start coughing and sneezing. This is not good for them. Locally contracted roofing sheets-house of 6ft long, 2 and half (2 2/2) feet wide and 2 and a half (2 2/2) feet high with space in front made with wire mesh of one square feet for ventilation has been used to brood 100-150 chicks. Open the cover (top) during the hot day.

Poor brooding can cause 50-60% cases of chicks.

❖ When chicks crowd up at the edge of the house it indicates they are hot. But it they crown up around the source of heat it indicates that they are cold and when evenly distributed in the space provided, it shows they are warm enough.

❖ Excessive cold can lead to paralysis and finally death while excessive heat can lead to dehydration and finally death.

❖ In colder month you need 200 watts bulb to 50chick but in warm months one 200 watts bulbs can do for 100 chicks.

❖ Cement or newspapers can be used to cover the wood shavings in the brooding area for at least 10days. Remove the paper after the 10th day of brooding.

You may have to put the chicks on Glucose depend on how far the chicks must have traveled before getting to you.

Sanitation

❖ A clean environment is essential. Remove cob-webs, clean dust from the house and cut grasses around the pen house.

❖ To control diseases when visiting a house, movement should be from younger to older and from healthy to sick houses.

❖ No visitor should be allowed any how into the house (especially co-farmers) to avoid the spread of disease.

❖ Provide a foot bath (container at the entrance containing water with disinfectant) for feet dipping before entering and while coming out of poultry house, cloths, boots (shoe) for use in poultry should he made available and such should be charged while leaving premises. In case it is difficult to maintain footbath with disinfectant you can provide rubber slippers to be used only when entering the poultry house Burn or buy birds to avoid disease spread in the environment.

❖ Remove sick birds from flock to isolate pens to check diseases spread.

❖ Disinfectant to be used should be recommended by experts.

❖ Weekly preparation in containers at the entrance for dipping feet helps to kill germs from the legs.

❖ After a stubborn diseases condition, ask your vet for the right disinfectant eg. Potassium permanganate is good for viral disease control.

Vaccination Programme

Many poultry diseases can be prevented by good management practices, including sanitation, adequate feeding, well-ventilated houses, etc. However, some poultry diseases, particularly viral and bacterial disease, could easily and rapidly spread, and can result in a high death toll. The most reasonable approach to the control of these diseases is by vaccination.

❖ To protect is better than curing. An adage that has its full interpretation as far as poultry business is concern. The effect of diseases outbreak is life lasting in poultry.

❖ Birds will hardly reach their original designed potential once they suffer am outbreak.

❖ Vaccination is the only way out. No substitute for sound vaccinations. If there is no money for feed in none-laying birds or in a broiler farm, you can skip a day without feed. It is safer than failure to vaccinate.

❖ Use anti-stress or vitamins/mineral mix for 2 days before and after vaccination.

❖ Use powdered milk to de-chlorinate water giving water soluble vaccines only water (chemically tested) with no chlorine will require no milk make sure two weeks elapsed between the first and second Gumboro. Also provide adequate number of drinkers when giving vaccine in water to avoid overdosing and or under dosing. I suggest that you provide one plastic drinker for every 25 birds during water vaccination.

❖ Don't over excite birds within the period of vaccination.

❖ Do not change house immediately after vaccination.

❖ Immediately after any vaccination, give birds water with some common salt in it. Use it at a dose of I gram per liter of water or 1 teaspoonful into a gallon of water.

- ❖ Ask your vet for local vaccination program (such as the one presented below for those in Northern Region) because disease pattern differs from places to places.
- ❖ Certain vaccines are not advised for laying birds. So consult your vet in all cases.

Notes when vaccinating younger chicks (less than 10days old) through drinking water, make sure you withdraw water for nothing less than 16 hours to make them thirsty enough. But for those more than 10days old 10-12 hour water starvation is enough depending on where the farm is and the time of the year.

Guide to Incubation & Hatching

Incubating your own hatching eggs at home can be one of the most rewarding parts of raising chickens. This guide contains helpful information for the novice and experienced Hatcher alike. I must warn you, however: it's addictive! Once you begin hatching your own baby chicks, you may never be able to stop...

Mothering chicken eggs is not for everyone, but if you think it might be your calling, here's how to do it.

Choosing between an incubator and a hen

a.   Hen Considerations

Once you have determined that you're flexible and determined enough to try hatching eggs, you must decide whether you would like to hatch them in an incubator or instead hatch them under a broody hen.

Why a Hen?

Reasons to have a broody hen hatch eggs for you include first of all that it's simply wonderful to see a mama hen with her babies - it's fun to see them ride on her back and peek out from beneath her wings. It's adorable the way she will teach them what is good to eat, and how to scratch and forage for food. It is the most natural way for baby chicks to be raised.

Plus, it's practical: when a hen is incubating eggs, you needn't worry about the power going out and ruining the eggs in your incubator. There are no concerns about the temperature and humidity being right. You needn't worry about a heat lamp in the brooder, because the mama will keep them warm. It is, all around, a fabulous remedy to many of the things hatchers often worry about.

She needs to be "Broody"

Your hen may not be broody when you need her to be, and there is no way to "make" her go broody. Timing is everything. Broodiness is a hormonal condition. In fact, the hormone that relates to ovulation in humans (as well as to breast milk production) is the same one that causes a hen to become broody: it is an increase in prolactin that causes incubation behavior.

We have our own theories about how to increase prolactin levels in a hen based on studies of other animals but no one has done any research on hens, yet. (Any takers?) That said, studies of other animals have shown that high levels of calcium are associated with high prolactin levels; one wonders if the reverse is true: whether an increased intake of calcium will cause higher prolactin levels (and thus incubation behavior). My little Silkie hen, so inclined to broodiness, goes broody nearly every time I refill the oyster shell in the coop!

You'll Need to Invest in Special Equipment

You will need a brooder. You will still need some special equipment, even for a broody hen. It is not the best idea to let her hatch her babies right in the coop with the rest of the flock. The reason is that often she chooses the "favorite" nest to go broody in.

This is probably not such a big deal, except that she may have other hens crowding in and laying eggs on top of her. The crowding can cause your precious eggs to break, and having new eggs added to the clutch later in incubation can mean that toward the end, she may be sitting on too many eggs to effectively cover and incubate them, so some could die.

Sometimes eggs can get broken or knocked out of the nest by accident, even if there is no competition for nest space with other hens. In the case of a broody hen, the success or failure of incubation is out of your hands, and depends on your hen.

For all these reasons, i recommend providing your broody hen with a safe "broody coop" where she can sit on her eggs in peace and hatch her babies without being accosted. Plus, if the chicks hatch in the main coop with the rest of the flock, the other birds may well attack the newcomers! While mother will try to protect them, the best scenario is simply to prevent this from happening in the first place by giving them a safe place until they are larger and mother has recovered a bit.

One Dozen Maximum

The last reason you may not want to have a broody hen hatch your eggs is that a hen can only reliably hatch a few eggs at a time. Bantams can't easily hatch more than six or seven large eggs at a time. (They will be able to cover more eggs if they are smaller.) Large fowl birds may be able to hatch 10 or 12 at the very most, depending on the size of the bird and the size of the eggs.

When you choose to hatch under a hen, you are limited as to the number of eggs you can set. If you are hatching in quantity you may want to try incubating two dozen or more at once. When that is the case, a single broody hen will just not do.

The Best Breed for your Needs

If you are decided on a hen, however, you will want to know how to choose the best or your hatching needs. Some breeds will never go broody, so if you are waiting for your favorite to get in the mood for hatching, it may be a very long wait! My favorite broody breeds for hatching eggs include:

1. Silkie

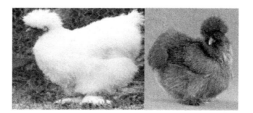

The Silkie (pictured above) is, hands down, the Broody Queen of the chicken world. As a bantam breed, it's rather petite but incredibly docile, considered by some to be the chicken version of a lapdog. It's easygoing nature and soft, fur-like feathers makes it a perfect chicken mama. These ornamental birds are not easy to find and also make a great pet chicken for kids.

Unlike other chicken breeds, these birds can double as pets and attract high prices.

2. Cochin

The Cochin hen runs a tight race with the Silkie for the Broody Crown and comes up just short. A Chinese breed, just like the Silkie, the Cochin is known for being big, sweet, fluffy and docile. It's available in a variety of colors and feather patterns, including Frizzled. Although it doesn't lay as well as some of the dual-purpose breeds, it makes a fantastic mother and an all around great pet chicken.

3. Orpington

This English dual-purpose breed gets its name from the town of Orpington near London, where it originated. It's incredibly cold-hardy, thanks to its fluffy, loose feathers that make it look heftier than it actually is. The Orpington is also a gentle bird with a sweet personality. Unlike Silkies and Cochins, Orpingtons are first-rate layers of light brown eggs. The breed is recognized in several color varieties, with Buff, a beautiful golden-yellow color, being the most popular. It's a favorite of family flocks and a perfect breed for children to care for, due to its gentle nature.

4. Brahma

The Brahma is a gentle giant and another wonderfully sweet and broody breed. Quiet, calm and even-tempered, it's exceptionally cold hardy and the hens are great layers during cold weathers. Because of its feathered legs and shanks, it's best not to keep this breed in excessively wet or muddy regions, as moisture can cling to the feathers, leading to frostbite on the toes.

5. Sussex

The Sussex is a reliable brooder. It's friendly and very curious by nature. The Speckled variety has a unique feather pattern that effectively camouflages the bird from most predators - a boon when free-ranging.

There are plenty of other breeds that will go broody, but keep in mind that just because a hen goes broody, it is no guarantee she will be a good mother. For instance, some hens will go broody, but will not stay on the nest consistently, so few if any eggs will hatch.

Some hens are so startled when the eggs finally hatch, that mother hen may attack the new chicks, not knowing what to do with these invaders, where before she had nice, round, warm (quiet) eggs! It is not a good scenario.

Some hens will go out on their own, leaving the little chicks behind. Then, they may be "done" raising the chicks quite early, when the babies still may benefit from a mother's protection. If you have a choice, make sure to pick a good broody breed. If you find you have a hen that is a good brooder AND mother, thank your lucky stars, and be sure to let her hatch your eggs at every opportunity.

B. Incubator Considerations

If a hen will not work for you for whatever reason, you may want an incubator. Be sure to have your chosen incubator on hand before ordering eggs. The last thing you want is to have your eggs ready to set in three days, but have to wait ten more for your incubator to arrive! Good planning is the key.

Choosing to use an incubator is a different proposition than choosing a broody hen altogether. With an incubator, you should be prepared for the anxiety of waiting twenty-one days for your babies, coupled with the fact that YOU and ONLY you are absolutely responsible for whether or not they hatch!

Worse, many people just won't "get" why you may be so anxious! Three weeks certainly doesn't seem like a long time to wait... not until you're the broody mom hatching your eggs. Once you begin incubation, chances are good that you will be anxious for three full weeks! When I'm incubating, I quake every time I have a storm, because if the power goes out, it can adversely affect how many eggs hatch! If it goes out for very long, it can even kill the babies in the shell. I have a generator to supply power when AEDC (national grid) power is off.

I have a few tips for making sure your eggs will make it through the entire incubation cycle:

❖ If AEDC keeps a list of people to be notified about scheduled outages in your area, request to be on it.

- ❖ Make sure anyone who has the opportunity to interact with your incubator is informed about how important it is not to lift the lid, much less turn off the power.

- ❖ If you have young children, make sure they understand what's at stake. If they're too young to understand that, then be sure to put your incubator out of reach. Many young children have been known to try cracking the eggs early so they can see the baby chicks they have been told are hiding inside!

- ❖ If you have dogs, cats or other pets, make sure your incubator is in a place it won't be bothered. It's no fun to discover that your puppy now knows just how delicious eggs are at the expense of all your fertile eggs!

- ❖ In general, it's best to keep your incubator on a sturdy surface that won't be knocked or stepped on, and in a place that has relatively stable temperatures, out of the way of drafts and direct sunlight.

Depending on how many eggs they accommodate and how automated they are, Incubators run from around N50,000 for the homesteader up to N250,000 and more for commercial scale incubators.

With top-of-the-line incubators, you put in an egg, close the door and out pops the chick three weeks later. You can also go the DIY route, which saves money, but is almost as much work as sitting on the eggs yourself. No matter how fancy or jerry-rigged, all incubators must accomplish a few basic things:

Temperature: The eggs need to be kept at 99.5 degrees at all times; just one degree higher or lower for a few hours can terminate the embryo.

Humidity: 40 to 50 percent humidity must be maintained for the first 18 days; 65 to 75 percent humidity is needed for the final days before hatching.

Ventilation: Egg shells are porous, allowing oxygen to enter and carbon dioxide to exit; incubators need to have holes or vents that allow fresh air to circulate so the fetuses can breathe.

Homemade versions usually involve some sort of insulated box - a cheap Styrofoam cooler will do. An adjustable heating pad or a light bulb on a dimmer switch will suffice for the heat source and a pan of water with a sponge in it will make the air humid. Low-end commercial incubators don't amount to much more than this, but the more you pay, the more automated the temperature and humidity controls will be.

A high-quality thermometer and hygrometer (a device to measure humidity) are the most important tools of incubation; cheap models are usually not accurate enough. If you're not working with an incubator that has these instruments built in, opt for a combo thermometer/hygrometer with an external display. These have a sensor that goes inside the incubator with a LED screen on the outside that shows the temperature and humidity readings without having to open the incubator and ruin your carefully calibrated environment.

One time-saving feature is a device to rotate the eggs automatically. Much of the fussing that a hen does over her eggs comes from an evolutionary instinct to constantly move them about. The finely tuned ecosystem inside a chicken egg is kept in balance by constantly changing the position of the egg. High-end incubators have a built-in egg turning device, but there are also standalone egg turners that can be placed inside a homemade incubator to do the job. Or, you can rotate manually.

The incubator should be placed in a location with the least possible fluctuation in temperature and humidity throughout the day - a basement is ideal, a sunny window is not.

Find Fertile Eggs

If you already have a flock of hens with a cock, the majority of the eggs they lay will be fertile. Make sure that you have 1 cock for every 5 hens for high chances of fertilized eggs. Collect them as soon as possible after laying and transfer to the incubator.

If you don't already have chickens, find a friend or a nearby farmer who does and ask if you can buy some fertile eggs. Also big chicken farms in Nigeria are a good place to get a wide variety of fertilized eggs. Some feed stores sell fertile eggs and there are many suppliers that sell fertilized eggs.

The closer to home, the better the egg source. The jostling about and fluctuations in temperature and humidity that occur during transport are hard on the developing fetus. Hatching rates on eggs straight from the coop are often in the 75 to 90 percent range; with far transported eggs, there is no guarantee that any will hatch.

When picking eggs to incubate, use those that are clean, well-formed and full-size. Above all, do not clean the eggs - there is a naturally occurring coating that is vital to the success of the embryo. Wash your hands before handling and be as gentle as possible, as the embryos are extremely susceptible to damage from sudden movements.

Ideally, the eggs are transferred directly to the incubator, but it's possible to store them in egg cartons if needed. Kept at temperatures between 50 and 60 degrees and 75 percent humidity, the development of the eggs can be delayed for up to ten days without sacrificing the viability of the embryos. However, they must be stored with the fat side of the egg pointed up to keep the embryo alive.

It takes 21 days on average for an egg to hatch once incubation begins. Before placing the eggs inside, turn on the heat source and measure the temperature and humidity over a 24-hour period, making adjustments as necessary to create the optimal environment. If the humidity is too high or low, use a sponge with more or less surface area to adjust it. Raise and lower the temperature of the heat source in tiny increments until the thermometer reads 99.5.

Once the incubator is functioning properly, it's just a matter of maintaining the environment until the chicks hatch. Place the eggs on their side in the incubator, close the door and check the levels religiously to make sure nothing goes askew. Water may have to be added to the pan occasionally to keep the humidity up. At day 18, add more water to boost the humidity level.

If you're going to turn the eggs yourself, there is a standard method to mimic the efforts of a hen:

☐ Draw an 'X' on one side of the egg and an 'O' on the other to keep track of which eggs have been turned.

☐ At least three times a day, gently turn the eggs over; more frequent turning is even better, but the number of turns per day should be odd (3,5,7 etc.) so that the eggs are never resting on the same side for two consecutive nights. Experts also recommend alternating the direction of turning each time - the goal is to vary the position of the embryo as much as possible.

☐ Continue turning until day 18, but then leave the eggs alone for the last few days.

Hatching

In the final days before hatching the eggs may be observed shifting about on their own as the fetus becomes active. The chick will eventually peck a small hole in the large end of the egg and take its first breath. It is normal at this point for the chick to rest for six to 12 hours while its lungs adjust before continuing to hatch. Resist the urge to help with the hatching process - it's easy to cause injury!

Once the chick is free from the egg, let it dry off in the warmth of the incubator before moving it a brooder, where it will spend the first weeks of its life. Since we have learnt about brooding, I think it is good to have a case study of someone who has tried hatching his/her own chicks at home.

Chick Hatching: Case Study

About a kilometre from Sabatia Eye Clinic along the Chavakali-Kapsabet Road in Vihiga County, there sits the Paradise Farm. From the name, one conjures up images of an expansive crop farm with several trees and beautiful sites akin to the Garden of Eden.

Owner Victor Obimbo, however, keeps poultry and runs a hatchery specializing in day-old chicks. He rears over 700 Kari Improved Indigenous breed chicken in a 60 by 45 feet coop.

"Right now I have 580 hens and the rest are cockerels. There were over 1,000 of them but over Christmas, I sold 500 cockerels to three community based organizations in Siaya County for breeding purposes at Sh1,200 each. This also helped me reduce their number."

Obimbo started the agribusiness in December 2014 after attending a series of trainings offered by officers from Nigeria Agricultural and Livestock Research Organisation (Kalro), Kakamega.

"One of the things I learned from Kalro was how to operate the incubator and set the temperature. For the first 18 days, I set temperature and humidity at 37.8 degrees Celsius and 60-65 respectively. From this day onwards, I set the former and the latter at 37.5 degrees Celsius and 70-75 respectively," says Obimbo, adding that for one to run a hatchery, you must have a licence from the Nigeria Veterinary Board, which is renewed annually.

Thereafter, he bought 1,000 Kari Improved chicks from Naivasha at Sh100 each. "I used over Sh.500,000 from my savings to build the housing unit, buy feeds, drinkers and other equipment."

In March last year, he added another 1,000 chicks to increase the parent stock and achieve his dream of running a hatchery after he had acquired six incubators.

"My incubators have an egg capacity of 2,160 each. My hatching rate is 1,700 chicks out of the 2,100 eggs I incubate each week," says 48-year-old, adding he collects about 400 eggs every day.

The best hen to cockerel ratio in poultry breeding is 1:7, according to him.

"Most farmers overwork their cockerels and this lowers the quality of chicks," says Obimbo, who also farms maize and wheat in large-scale in Kitale and Narok counties.

BIGGEST EXPENSE

In a month, he spends approximately Sh.37,000 on commercial poultry feeds, what the farmer says is his biggest expense. "I buy about 10kg bags of layers mash and five bags of growers mash in a month, with each going for Sh.2,400 and for Sh.2,500 respectively. I am yet to learn how to make my own feeds but that is the route I want to take to cut costs."

From day-old to about eight weeks, the farmer feeds them on chick mash, which is very essential in growth of feathers. At eight to 19 weeks, the chicks are fed on growers mash and finally the layers mash completes the meal. "Before I sell the chicks, I give them Mareks vaccine and follow a vaccination programme for diseases such as Newcastle, Gumboro and fowl pox."

I won't tell you how much he earns from his hatching business since i guess you have already done the calculations and estimations. Maybe a hint, he sells the chicks at N.80-100.

Purchasing Day Old Chicks

You have to keep in mind some essential information before selecting the layer, Indigenous breed or broiler hens for your poultry farming business. You have to select those breeds which are suitable for your poultry farming business and can produce well in your area. Read below for selecting proper breeds for your business.

❖ For commercial eggs production, you have to choose highly productive laying hens correctly.

❖ All type of hens does not produce equal number of eggs.

❖ The chosen breeds must have good production capability e.g eggs, meat or dual purpose.

❖ If your chosen breed contains the desired characteristic and have a reputation for egg production, then that breed is suitable for your business.

❖ Always purchase healthy chicks from a famous and popular hatchery. You can see their catalog before purchasing.

Caring for Baby Chicks

Just like puppies, baby chicks are unbelievably adorable and loveable. And just like puppies, they're a handful! I totally recommend it for anyone looking for a poultry flock. This section covers all the basics of baby chick care.

Baby chicks can be purchased at a poultry hatchery or garden/farm supply store.

Clearing Your Schedule

Baby chicks require constant care and monitoring, so make sure your schedule is clear for the first 4 weeks! Don't plan on vacations or even day trips unless you have a seasoned baby chick worker on standby. Make sure you or a member of your family are available to check on them *at least* 5 times a day.

Deciding Where They're Going to Live

You can keep young chicks almost anywhere: their small size makes them easy to handle! They grow quickly, though, and by the time they're three or four weeks old they'll be taking up a lot of space and making a big mess, so preparing a living space for them is actually quite important. The good news is that you can transfer them to their outside coop at 4-5 weeks of age, so you won't have to deal with the mess for too long... I will talk more on that below.

Ideally you'll have a garage, basement or another predator-proof and draft-proof environment that's not in your main living space. Why not the main living space? Baby chicks, just like grown chickens, love to "scratch" their bedding materials, which creates a very fine dust that gets everywhere. The older they get, the more dust they make. Baby chicks also have a smell... It's not decidedly bad, nor do we find it overwhelming, but you may not want it in your house.

If you don't have a garage, worNop or basement in which to keep them, pick the next best option. Do you have a three season porch where it won't get too cold? A spare bedroom whose surfaces you can cover? If none of the above does your kitchen have an eat-in area not too close to prep surfaces that you're willing to sacrifice for a few weeks? Choose the best possible option keeping in mind that wherever you keep them, they must be safe from predators and drafts.

I remember when i was a kid in the 1970s, my dad could raise day old chicks in one of the vacant bedrooms in the house and lower the light bulb so that they could get warmth.

8 things you must consider when buying day-old chicks

1.   Process of production of day old chicks

Poultry and poultry houses are known to harbor bacteria that cause zoonotic infections. Such include salmonellosis and shigellosis. Such bacteria like salmonella can breach the shell integrity into the egg-causing early infections.

2. Research

Due to these bacteria, extreme hygiene has to be practiced at the hatchery including fumigation of eggs before hatching. This eliminates all pathogens to ensure hatched chicks are healthy. The eggs are also cleaned to remove gross dirt before incubation.

If this is not done, one may buy day-old chicks from an unapproved source then few days or weeks later, despite you doing everything right, the birds might come down with one infection and this could be the source of your problems. If a hatchery manages to posses these characteristics then it meets the bare minimum required to produce good quality chicks. With this in place, then the hatchery must be inspected by the veterinary authorities and licensed to be in the business of chick production.

Most farmers are duped by unscrupulous dealers who invoke names of trusted brands in the market. A physical visit at the hatchery is therefore a must to also examine their health and history record.

3. Vaccination and health status of chicks

Before purchasing chicks, a farmer must confirm if they have been vaccinated against common poultry viral diseases such as Marek's disease. If the birds are not vaccinated in the hatchery, then one must have a veterinary surgeon on standby who would give the vaccinations to the chicks as soon as they get to you to prevent diseases or death.

4. Ecological region

High breed chicken is highly sensitive to extreme fluctuations in environmental temperatures. An aspiring farmer is therefore advised to purchase birds from hatcheries within their ecological area. Chicks bred in areas with low environmental temperatures are likely to die of heat stress if taken to areas with high environmental temperatures.

The knowledge about temperature changes will also help a farmer prepare himself adequately for energy needs like solar, electricity or cooling gadgets in case of extreme heat.

5. Time

Time is also an important factor when buying day-old chicks. This is because day old chicks require a lot of care and attention especially in the first five weeks of purchase. Therefore, you must clear out your schedule and ensure that you would have time to care for them when you buy them.

6. Size

When you buy day-old chicks, they are usually so small that 1,000 of them can fit into a tiny space. But you shouldn't allow this initial size deceive you; as they grow older, they begin to consume a lot of space and if you didn't do proper space planning at the point of buying day-old chicks, you would face a lot of space challenges.

7. Means of transport

Since they are very delicate, it is important to use special containers when transporting day-old chicks from their current location to the destination you want to send them. Use containers that are hard on the outside and soft on the inside.

When the inside of the container is soft it will act as shock absorber to protect the chicks from bruising. Day old chicks are very delicate and find it difficult to sustain injuries when they are bruised and they may die. The container should be put in a place that will prevent vigorous shaking and movement because when that happen your chicks will crash into each other and some will get their limbs and other parts of their body broken.

8. Ventilation during transit

The type of transport you use to carry the chicks should be well ventilated to enable proper breathing of the chicks which is extremely crucial during movement. The portions allocated for the ventilation shouldn't be too much as to expose the chicks to strong wind as it can cause death through suffocation.

Once all the desired factors are in place, the farmer should be able to have all the structures and equipment ready for the take off of the farm.

Creating a Suitable Living Environment

This is the one of the most important part of raising happy, healthy chicks. The baby chick house is also known as the "brooder". Baby chicks need to be protected from drafts but still have adequate ventilation. This can be in the form of a cardboard box with holes for ventilation, a single-faced corrugated cardboard roll, 12" or higher, a large plastic storage bin, or even a kiddie pool!

All of the above have been used with success. Whatever housing solution you go with, make sure it provides 2 square feet per chick. It sounds like an awful lot, but as they get older (and bigger) you'll realize why this is necessary.

A heat source

Baby chicks need to be kept pretty hot. The first week of their lives they require an air temperature of 95 degrees, the second week 90 degrees, and so on - going down by 5 degrees per week until they're ready to transition to "outside".

A poultry gas brooder heater and 250-watt infrared heat lamp is the best way to achieve this, placed right in the middle of their living area and suspended off the ground. The height of the light will depend on what it takes to achieve your target temperature.

I recommend a red heat bulb for a few reasons: one, with a bright white light constantly glaring it can be hard for them to sleep. The red light is darker and provides them some respite. Two, red lights help prevent them from pecking one another.

Pay close attention to how your chicks behave. If they're all crowded together directly under the heat source, they're cold. Lower the heat lamp or add another one. If they're around the edges of the brooder avoiding the heat and each other like the plague, they're too hot! Raise the heat lamp. A happy flock will happily be exploring all around the brooder.

And please do not listen to anyone that tells you a regular old 60 watt bulb will suffice! I have seen chicks die from this bad advice. They really need a lamp intended to produce heat, and as we've mentioned, I recommend the 250-watt variety and Lenarc-phil poultry heater.

Absorbent bedding

Baby chicks are big poopers, so make sure to line the floor of their housing unit with an absorbent material. The best, I think, is to spread wood shavings/ saw dust about 1" thick.

Avoid the urge to use newspaper! It's not a good absorbent and the slippery surface can lead to a permanent deformity called "splayed leg" which can ultimately result in the other chickens picking on the affected bird to death.

Many people also swear by paper towels, changed often. (DON'T use cedar shavings, no matter what friends or your local feed store tell you: the aromatic oils will irritate your chicks' lungs, and make them more susceptible to respiratory problems later in life.)

A drinker / water disher

I recommend you don't try to use a dish, a rabbit drinker, or anything you have just

"laying around". Baby chicks have special needs when it comes to water. Dishes can make it easy for chicks to drown, and they'll certainly do naughty things like walk in it, spill it, kick their bedding materials into it, and poop in it -- meaning you'll have to change it constantly.

Rabbit drinkers aren't preferable, either, because not enough chicks can access it at once. For the best results, i recommend you use a chick drinker i explained in chapter 8. They come in a number of different sizes and shapes, all basically sufficient.

Keep in mind that even with the best drinker, they'll still kick bedding materials into it and find ways to poop in it from time to time. Raising the drinker off the ground somewhat will help (starting their second week of life), but no matter what they're going to get that water messy, so plan on changing it a few times a day.

A feeder

Once again, I recommend you resist the temptation to use a dish or bowl for feeding your chicks. They're messy, and they'll jump in and kick the feed all over the place, poop in it, and the worst case scenario: they'll tip it over and trap a baby underneath. (This has happened!) Spend those few extra shillings and buy a "real" baby chick feeder, or borrow one from a friend. They come in many shapes and sizes, just as I explained in chapter 8.

Bonus: Roosting Poles

Chickens love to roost on poles or branches when they're resting. You don't have to provide your brood roosting poles, but they'll be even happier if you do. I like half inch diameter wooden dowels. Try them about 5 inches off the ground. (They may like it so much, so that they don't roost on top of your feeder and drinker!)

Feed

Fortunately this one doesn't require much thought! Suppliers have formulated special feed complete with everything baby chicks need. It's called "starter feed" and comes in either "crumbles" or "mash" (referring to how ground down it is). Either is fine.

The only thing to know is that if you've had your chicks vaccinated against Coccidiosis, they'll need an un-medicated feed. If not, or if you've only had them vaccinated for Marek's Disease, medicated feed is a great way to keep them healthy those first few months.

A question I commonly get is how long to feed baby chicks "starter feed" for before switching to a feed called "grower" or "chick grower". The answer is: it all depends! Each manufacturer formulates their feed differently, so read the label and follow their instructions. Some only recommend the starter for 4 weeks before moving onto grower; some combine both together in a "starter/grower" feed that can last up to 16 weeks, etc.

Farmers also ask me whether they can feed their chicks scraps, or worms and other bugs from the garden... Small amounts of vegetable/dairy should be fine for the chicks (and they'll love it!), and the same goes with bugs and worms. But consider those like dessert, not the main course. Starter feeds contain everything chicks need to survive and thrive, and filling them up with too much of the "other stuff" can throw off their nutritional balance.

Finally, people want to know how much food they should give their birds. The answer is: as much as they want! Don't ration it. Give your birds 24/7 access to all the food they can eat. They're not like dogs. They'll self-regulate.

Grit

Ever heard the saying "scarce as a hen's teeth"? That's right, chickens don't have them! Instead they eat tiny pebbles and store them in their "crop". When the food enters their crop, the pebbles grind it up to make digestion easier.

For baby chicks, sand, parakeet gravel or canary gravel, available at your local agrovet shop, will suffice. You can either sprinkle this in their feed or provide it in a small cup or bowl.

Avoid giving your chicks house building and construction sand. Your chicks will get infection from the contaminated or disinfected sand.

Netting for the top

Although most grown chickens are pretty pathetic flyers, young chicks are much more capable. If your brooder is only 12 inches high, don't be surprised if you find your week-old chicks perching on top of it! To prevent this, i recommend you cut a section of deer netting or chicken wire just big enough to drape over your brooder, or use a 2-foot-high brooder box to increase the length of time before they're able to "fly the coop".

Bringing Your Baby Chicks Home

First things first: find out what day your chicks will be arriving. When you get them home, be prepared: one or two may have died in transporting or may be on their "way out". This isn't due to disease. Some chicks are born less hardy than others and can't withstand the stress and cold temperatures involved in transporting them around the country.

Most hatcheries, in fact, prepare for that by including an extra bird or two for free. (Beware, though, as some hatcheries will throw in broilers even if you didn't order them! Ensure if they include extras, they only include a bird of the same breed and sex as one you've ordered.)

Care for the weak birds as best as you can, and bury the dead birds as you would any other pet. Also, call the hatchery right away to let them know if a bird dies. They'll usually either give you a partial refund or a discount on your next order so long as you notify them within 24 - 48 hours of arrival.

A note for parents ordering chicks

Since baby chicks do die from time to time in transporting, I recommend that if you've got young children:

❖ Do not tell them when the chicks are coming.

❖ Do not tell them how many chicks you've ordered, and

❖ Do not have them with you when you inspect the box for the first time.

This way if there are any losses, you can deal with them without the kids ever being the wiser. Losses are not common, but when they do happen they can be devastating to little ones.

Important health notes

Pasting Up

As you move your baby chicks from their shipping box into their brooder kit (which you've set up and heated in advance, of course!), check them for "pasting up", a condition in which their droppings cake up and block their vent opening, preventing them from passing any more droppings. This problem will be pretty obvious; you won't have to go poking around their insides to see it. The dried poop will be stuck to their outside, totally or partially covering their vent.

This is a deadly condition and must be dealt with immediately. To clear the blockage, use a warm, wet paper towel to soften the poop blocking the vent. It should then be relatively easy to remove. To make sure your chick doesn't get chilled during this process, you may want to do this near a heat source and make sure to keep the wet paper towel warm.

In bad cases where the water is just not penetrating the mass to soften it, you may have to dunk the chick's rear in warm water before it will loosen up enough to remove it, and sometimes you will CAREFULLY have to use tweezers. Your chick will complain, loudly, but stand fast in your determination knowing that the chick will die if you don't!

Once you've succeeded, dry the chick off with a blow dryer and immediately return her to the brooder kit with the others. Be sure to wash and sanitize your hands thoroughly when you're done; you've just been handling poop, after all! And keep checking the birds that presented with this problem, for it often returns throughout the first week.

Immediate access to water

Your new brood will need water right away. Watch them carefully once you've transferred them to their new home. If they aren't finding the water, pick an especially spritely one and gently put its beak into the water. This should be enough to teach them - once one chick's drinking the others are sure to follow!

The same goes with the food: make sure they're finding it. If not, show them. Resist the temptation to feed your chicks water with a syringe. This can cause death by drowning, even if you're very careful about it. Just gently dip their beaks in water. If one is still not drinking, chances are it is struggling to stay alive and may not make it. So don't force it to drink with a syringe.

The Umbilical Cord

Some baby chicks will arrive to you with an intact, attached umbilical cord. It looks like a very thin black string, attached to their rear. For heaven's sake, don't pull it! It's not "pasting up"! Just leave it alone. It will fall off within a day or two. Pulling it can really injure them.

Ongoing Chick Care

Keep checking up on your chicks several times a day. They'll be doing naughty things like kicking up their bedding into the feed and water, and you'll have to clean up after them. (Don't forget, they need round-the-clock access to all the food and water they can get their beaks on!) Also pay close attention to their behavior. I said it before and I'll say it again because it's key: If they're crowded together directly under the heat source, they're cold. Lower the heat lamp or add another one. If they're around the edges of the brooder avoiding the heat and each other like the plague, they're too hot! Raise the heat lamp. Not getting this right can be the death of young chicks.

Changing Bedding

For sanitary purposes and to keep their area from stinking, change their bedding at least once a week. We used to throw ours in the compost pile where it's happily turned into rich earth.

Heating over time

Don't forget that your baby chicks need less and less heat as time goes by. By their 2nd week the heat can be reduced 5 degrees to 90, by the 3rd week by another 5 degrees to 85 and so on. However, this is just a guideline. Continue tuning into their behavioral cues as described above and you'll know how to tweak their heat.

Also, keep in mind that some of your chicks will develop faster than others, requiring less heat, while the "runty" ones will want to be closer to the heat lamp. Make sure your heating set-up gives each chick the choice of how much heat is comfortable to them (in other words, don't create a uniform temperature by putting the heat lamp inside the box and then covering the box!)

Dealing with kids & chicks

If you've got kids or you're planning on bringing kids over to see the chicks, set the boundaries up front. Chicks are irresistibly sweet and cheeky kids tend to harass them. Make sure you watch the chicks; if they show signs of distress, be firm and return them to their brooder. Also, if you have chicks that are or were recently pasted up, please instruct your kids to let them be. Over-handling can prevent a chick that is "on the edge" from bouncing back (it can be the death of them!).

Growing... and growing!

As your chicks get older you'll understand why I recommended a minimum of 2 square feet of living space per bird. If you provided them less than that and your older chicks are pecking at one another, do expand their living quarters. Both you and the chicks will be much less stressed. And as mentioned above, if they start flying on top of their brooder box, a simple length of deer netting or chicken wire laid on top of their living quarters should prevent it!

"Outside" time

After the chicks are 2-3 weeks old, if it's warm outside and sunny, feel free to let them have a little "outdoor time"! Put them in a wire cage or erect some other temporary housing and place it in the sun, making sure they have access to water and shade if they need it. They'll absolutely love digging around in the grass.

But don't leave them unattended! At this age they're VERY good at flying and VERY susceptible to predators. Plus, if it's windy they'll get cold (and they'll let you know they're unhappy with their loud chirping). By 4-5 weeks of age your chickens are ready to move outside full-time. And thank goodness! As much as you love them, you'll be thrilled to get them out of your house. Read the next chapters to learn about chicken coop/housing requirements, how to transition them to their coop and how to care for them as they get older. Also, keep in mind that if you're purchasing a chicken coop e.g cages it can take three or more weeks to arrive, so you may want to have that squared away before you get the chicks!

Baby Chick FAQs (Frequently Asked Questions)

Q: How much food should I give my baby chicks?

A: As much as they want! We talked about this a little above, but in case you didn't catch it, chickens aren't like dogs -- they won't eat themselves to death. They'll only eat as much as they need. So go on, spoil them! Give them as much food as you can fit in your feeder. They won't over-eat it.

Q: Is "pasting up" REALLY a deadly condition?

A: You bet it is! "Pasting up" is described above: it's when droppings cake up and block a baby chick's vent opening, preventing them from passing any more droppings, and it must be dealt with immediately. Apply a warm, wet paper towel to their rears and then use a toothpick to *gently* clear the blockage, or in severe cases dunk the chick's rear in warm water so it softens up enough to remove it.

Dry her off and return her to the brooder kit with the other chicks, and keep an eye on her in the coming days to make sure the problem doesn't return.

Caring for Grown Chickens

Caring for pet or Indigenous breed chickens is pretty easy compared to commercial chickens like layers and broilers! They have the same needs as most any other animals. In this section I'll fill you in on daily, monthly, semi-annual and annual chores, as well as other nuances of chicken husbandry.

What to Do on a Daily Basis

❖ Keep feeders and drinkers full.

❖ Make sure the drinker is clean. Chickens will be less inclined to drink dirty water, and a dehydrated bird can *very quickly* become ill or die.

- ❖ Check to make sure they all look active, bright and healthy. If they aren`t, make an appointment with your vet.

- ❖ Collect and refrigerate eggs, pointy side down for maximum freshness.

- ❖ If you've opened the coop door to let your chickens out, always be sure to close and secure it at dusk (once they've all returned!) to make sure predators can't get in. (Tip: if you have a cell phone that allows you to set a recurring alarm, try that as a reminder.)

Keep in mind that you can leave your chickens alone (if they are few) for a few days provided they have enough food, water and space for the duration of your trip. The eggs they'll have laid in your absence should still be good to eat. Fresh eggs keep for several days without refrigeration. Surprised? Consider this: hens lay an average of 10-12 eggs per "clutch" (the group of eggs that a hen sits on to incubate). They lay one egg per day and at the end of a 10-12 day laying period they roll all the eggs together to incubate them. That means the egg laid on day 1 is still good enough on day 12 to become a living, breathing baby chick - so it should be good enough for you to eat too!

Egg Tip: Your eggs may have some slight traces of dirt or chicken feces on them. Resist the urge to scrub them clean! Outside the egg is a delicate membrane called the "bloom" that wards off bacteria and other foreign matter? Scrubbing will damage this membrane. If you're one of those Type A people that needs perfect-looking eggs, rub them with your fingers *very* gently under warm water. Then, wash your hands thoroughly.

What to Do on a Monthly Basis

☐   Change the bedding or always clean the coop and the nest. This is necessary for sanitary purposes. Excessive ammonia buildup is dangerous to poultry and can cause respiratory illness.

☐   Remove the feces. We put ours in the compost bin or use it as fertilizer.

What to do on a Bi-annual Basis

Twice a year you've got to really scrub your coop clean! Remove bedding, nest materials, feed and water containers. For a cleaner, i recommend a concoction of 1 part bleach, 1 part dish soap, and 10 parts water. A strong citrus cleanser will also do the trick.

After cleaning, rinse well and let dry before replacing with fresh bedding. Do the same with the feed and water containers: clean thoroughly and rinse well, and replace with a fresh supply. You should be able to do this all in a couple hours!

Foods Chickens Shouldn't Eat

One of the great benefits of having a chicken is they take care of your unwanted leftovers! There are a few foods they shouldn't eat, though (and thanks to my agribusiness friends for helping me beef up this list over the years!):

☐ Citrus fruits and peels (they can cause a drop in egg production)

☐ Bones

☐ Any large serving of meat, or meat that has gone bad

☐ Garlic and onion (unless you want your eggs tasting like them)

- [ ] Avocado skins and pits

- [ ] Raw potato skins

- [ ] Long cut grass

- [ ] Chocolate

Also, we hear from chicken pros that Morning Glories and Daffodils are poisonous to chickens, and even though chickens will generally know how to avoid them, you might just want to keep an eye on them around these plants.

How to Handle Chickens

Handing chickens is an art, and practice makes perfect! The key is finding the balance between being gentle and letting them know that no matter how much they wriggle or squirm, they're not getting away.

First, put your dominant hand (the hand you write with) on the middle of their back. If you're new to chickens, it's helpful to secure their wings as much as possible with your thumb and forefinger. (Pros don't need to secure their wings at all!) Your other hand will need to take their legs out of the equation. Secure one leg between your thumb and forefinger, and the other between the forefinger and middle finger of the same hand.

Then lift them, supporting the lower portion of their body with the heel of your hand and wrist. Your dominant hand should still be on their back. Once you've got them up, holding them close to your body will prevent further wriggling. And again, as you get better at this you won't need that hand on their backs!

Winter Precautions

During cold seasons, most farmers want to do the very best they can for their flock, and we often get ask me whether they should heat their coop during winter. My feeling is this isn't a good idea. Chickens adapt to the cold weather over time. Their body metabolism actually changes along with the seasons. When you heat your coop, the birds will never get used to the colder outside temperature so if the heat were to accidentally cut out causing a sudden change in temperature, you could literally lose your entire flock overnight. I've seen it happen.

That said, if you live in a really cold climate there are a few precautions you can take to make everyone's lives easier (by which i mean you and your birds!):

☐   Protect combs and wattles from frostbite by rubbing on petroleum jelly or another heavy moisturizer every few days.

☐   Make sure the water supply does not freeze! This is very important. Chickens cannot live long without fresh water. If you don't have electricity in your coop and therefore cannot provide a water heater, i recommend you bring the drinker into your house every night, and return it outside every morning. Check the water once or twice a day to make sure it's not frozen. (This may does not happen in Nigeria but it happens in USA and other European countries.)

Summer Precautions

Excessive heat is a real risk to birds. Make sure they have access to fresh, clean water at all times. Provide them a source of shade outside and as much ventilation as possible inside.

Note: Your hens may lay fewer eggs during heat waves. This is a sign of stress, but laying rates will return to normal once the heat has receded.

Fertilizers & "Turf Builders": Are They Safe?

Heck no! If your birds are free-ranging on your lawn, abstain from applying fertilizers or "turf builders". These products very often contain pesticides, herbicides and other harsh, nasty chemicals. Not only can these cause illness in your birds, but you don't want to be eating eggs containing these materials.

Part of the benefit of keeping chickens is the comfort of knowing that those fabulous, fresh, delicious eggs are safe for you, your family and customers. Fertilizers and turf builders negate all that.

That said, we understand the pressures of suburban life: if you can't be the only chump in the neighborhood with dandelions and various other weeds, i recommend you use organic fertilizers in the front yard and limit your birds to the back.

What to Do if Your Chickens Get Sick

Most chicken illnesses are curable if they're caught in time! If you suspect one of your chickens may be under the weather, take the precautionary measure of isolating it from the rest of the flock. This will help prevent illness from spreading. (And of course, make sure the isolated chicken has access to food and water!)

Second, make an appointment with your veterinarian right away. You need to find one that specializes in avian medicine or farm animals, and we recommend that you find the nearest one prior to getting chickens.

The following symptoms indicate illness AND more symptoms will be enlisted in future chapters:

1.   Mangy appearance

2.   Visible mites

3.   Abnormal stool, including blood, visible worms, diarrhea, droppings that are all white. (Normal stool is brown with a white cap.)

4.   Sneezing

5.   Loss of energy or depression

6.   Sudden, drastic reduction in position in pecking order

7.   Loss of appetite

8.   Stunted growth

For a more complete account of poultry illness, symptoms and cures, i recommend you read chapter 8.

A few things NOT to worry about:

- ❖ Your chickens' first eggs will be pretty pathetic! They'll be small, shells will be weak and some won't even have shells at all. Don't worry! This is not a sign of sickness.
- ❖ Your chickens will lose and re-grow their feathers once a year. This is called "molting" and is perfectly normal. They won't lay eggs during this time.

❖ A tiny speck of blood in an egg. This is normal. Don't worry about it. But if it becomes frequent, or if there is a significant amount of blood, that's another story.

Remember, the most important part of keeping your chickens healthy is disease prevention! Follow the care instructions and coop specifications above and you'll have a happy, healthy flock. However, as with any animal, there's still a chance of illness. Since you'll be checking on your birds daily, you'll catch the illness early and increase the chance of a positive outcome.

Dealing with Death

Losing a pet is always terrible, and chickens are no exceptions. If you've lost your bird due to old age or a predator attack, bury it as you would any other pet: a full funeral, bagpipes, the works. Dig a hole several feet underground to prevent anything from getting at the corpse. If, on the other hand, your bird displayed signs of illness or died suddenly, for no apparent reason, you'll need to investigate. Contact your veterinarian.

Chapter 10

Housing Your Hens

What is the Best Poultry Housing System?

The poultry business is one business that has empowered loads of entrepreneurs simply because of how profitable it is. Besides being a profitable business, it is also easy to setup especially if you are starting on a smaller scale and from a nice location. No doubt there are some challenges when it comes to running poultry farms and one of the challenges is that of proper housing system for your poultry.

There are a lot of factors that determine the effectiveness of a poultry housings system; factors such as ventilation system, flooring system, building insulation and fencing etc. The truth is that once a poultry farmer is able to get it right with the poultry housing system, then he can be rest assured that he wouldn't spend much when it comes to combating predators, disease causing organism and even unfavorable climatic conditions. The essence of a good poultry housing system is to minimize the cost of running your poultry farm and to maximize profits in the business.

Now the question is what is the best poultry housing system? As a matter of fact, the environment you intend starting your poultry farm and also the climatic condition of the area is a key factor that must be considered when designing your poultry housing system. You can also consider the species of the poultry, the age of the poultry and also the purpose you want the poultry farm to serve.

The basic poultry housing system for raising chickens, turkeys, ducks, and geese are brooder houses, batteries and accumulators; they serve different purpose. So the truth remains that the best poultry housing system depends on your purpose for going into poultry farm business. Now let us quickly consider some of the factors that will determine the best poultry housing system for you;

Choosing a Poultry Housing System –

Factors to Consider

A hen's coop is her castle! Proper housing is the key to happy, healthy birds, but building a chicken coop to the proper specifications is not as simple as it might seem. An adequate chicken coop design must:

1. Be predator-proof

Not just from the sides, but from above and below as well. Predators that would love chicken wings for dinner include but are not limited to raccoons, wild cats, coyotes and hawks. (Tip from a fellow chicken owner: be sure to select the right wire mesh. The holes in standard "chicken wire" are actually quite large. Yes, it will keep the chickens in, but raccoons can reach through those holes and do some nasty things... Not a pretty sight. I recommend one-half inch square "hardware cloth".)

2. Be secure from nasty rodents

Yes, rats! That will be attracted to the feed and droppings. Rodents are burrowing creatures, so you need to block them from slipping into the coop from below. If you coop doesn't have a floor, you need to bury small-mesh fencing down into the ground about 12" all around the coop.

3. Be breezy enough

In other to prevent respiratory diseases for which chickens are especially prone but not so drafty during winter that they freeze their tushes off, Chickens can withstand the cold so long as it's not drafty!

4. Be easy to clean so bugs and bacteria don't fester.

5. Provide "roosting poles" for your girls to sleep on (2" wide; rounded edges; allot 5-10" of space per bird side to side and 10" between poles if more than one is necessary; plus ladder-like grading so the pole furthest away is several inches higher than the closest).

6. Encourage egg-laying with 1 nest box for every four or nine chickens.

Nest boxes should be raised off the ground at least a few inches, but lower than the lowest roosting pole. They should also be dark and "out of the way" to cater to the hen's instinct to lay her eggs in a safe, place.

6. Be roomy

At least 4 square feet per bird if birds are able to roam freely during the day, and at least 10 square feet per bird if they are permanently confined.

7. Accommodate a feeder and drinker, which should hang 6-8" off the ground

8. Include a removable "droppings tray" under roosting poles for capture and easy disposal of droppings. (Or should we say for easy access to your lawn fertilizer?)

Similar to the coop, the sides of the attached chicken run, if you have one, should be buried 12" into the soil to keep predators and rodents from digging their way in. Once again, we recommend chicken wire fencing or half-inch hardware cloth. It's also my strong recommendation that you secure the top of the run with aviary netting or deer netting. This will keep wild birds (which can carry communicable diseases) out and provide further defense against sly predators.

9. The Age of the Poultry

Another factor that you should consider when designing housing system that will best suit your poultry business, is the age of the birds in your poultry. As was stated earlier, if you are dealing with younger chicks, then you should design your poultry housing system to suit them, also if you are dealing with older chickens, then you should have done your research with respect to some unique factors before making your choice on the kind of poultry housing system to design and build.

For instance; if one of the purpose of going into poultry farm business is to engage in the supply of eggs on a commercial level, then you can build poultry system that can facilitate safer and easy collections of eggs. As a matter of fact, you can build a cage that has more than 4 layers as long as you put other key factors such as light, ventilation and feeding into place before designing and building the cage to house your birds.

11. The Climatic Condition of the Environment You Intend Starting Your Poultry Farm

Another very important factor that should be consider before choosing a suitable poultry housing system is the climatic condition of the environment you intend starting your own poultry farm in. It is always advisable to go ahead and enquire from poultry owners in your area to know some of the climatic challenges that they go through before designing and building your own poultry housing system.

If you live in a region prone to cold, then you must build poultry system that is well insulated to provide the required heat for your birds. You should also consider proper ventilation system as well or else you will run into trouble trying to manage sickly birds. As a matter of fact, poor ventilation system is one major factor that contributes to the spread of various diseases in poultries.

12. The Location You Intend Starting Your Poultry Farm

The location you intend starting your poultry farm is yet another important factor that you must consider before choosing a poultry housing design. For example, if the location you choose to start your poultry farm can easily be accessed by predators, then you should consider fencing your poultry. There are various predators that can come after the birds in your poultry, it could be cats, it could be snakes, it could be dogs or even some wild animals that is why you must ensure that build a good fence that will help protect you birds.

Whichever choice you make regarding the best poultry housing system that can effectively fit into your plans of starting your poultry farm, just ensure that it is one that can give you easy access to feed your birds, treat them when they are sick and monitor their growth.

Tips and Requirements for a Good Poultry Housing System

If you have ever been to a good poultry farm, then you sure would realize that having a good poultry housing system is one way to ensure that things run smoothly in the farm as well as one factor that determines how healthy the animals might grow.

Therefore, if you have been in the business of poultry farming or have the penchant for poultry farming, it would really be expedient that you know the tips that are really needed for a good poultry housing system. When it comes to poultry farming, you have got to really take into account the availability of air in the environment.

Highlighted below are tips that would help with having a good poultry housing system and the steps that you would need to take to pull this off. If you are ready for the tips, then here goes;

a. Conduct a Research

This is one of the first most needful things that you have got to do. There is a whole lot of information that are available to you on the internet, especially those sites that are listed on the search engine. The role which a thorough and exhaustive research plays just cannot be emphasized. Some of the things that you would get to know about when you conduct research is that you will be able to get all the available options for a good poultry housing system and then you can make your choice.

b. A Good Poultry Housing System Should Have Easy Access

The hallmark of a good poultry housing system is that it should be designed in such a way that workers can easily move around the poultry without restrictions of obstruction. This is important especially when the birds are to be fed, given water and for effective cleaning of the poultry farm.

c. The Flooring / Bedding Must Be Comfortable for the Birds

The flooring / bedding of a good poultry housing system should be comfortable for the birds and should be safe for eggs as well. The truth is that if you do not get the bedding of your poultry right, eggs can easily get cracked and that won't be good for your business.

d. A Good Poultry Housing System Must Be Convenient To Clean

A good poultry housing system must be convenient to clean. It should be built in a way that every part of the poultry farm can be easily accessed by your cleaners. The truth is that hygiene is an important factor in the poultry business, especially if you want to minimize the death of your birds and spread of flu.

e. The Design of a Good Poultry Housing System Should Be Such That Eggs Don't Get cracked and are Easily Collected

Eggs are easily collected in a good poultry housing system. So ensure that the design of your own poultry farm is built in such a way that the eggs can easily be collected in good condition. If you have ever worked or visited a poultry farm, you will realize that an appreciable percent of the eggs normally get cracked. This is as a result of poor design. The safety of the eggs should be considered when building a poultry housing system.

f. A Good Poultry Housing System Must Have Good Lighting and Heating System

Another important tip that you must consider when building your poultry farm is the lighting and heating system. Birds like it when the environment is warm, it keep them healthy. So ensure that you install a proper lighting and heating system that can provide the adequate warmth needed by your birds. You can use translucent iron sheets to bring in light.

g. Proper Ventilation is a Key Factor for a Good Poultry Housing System

Another key factor that must be considered when building your poultry farm is the ventilation. The success of your poultry farm business to a large extent is dependent on the ventilation of the poultry farm. The truth is that if you don't have proper ventilation in your poultry farm, you are likely going to welcome easy spread of bird flu. So ensure that you design your poultry farm to allow for proper ventilation.

h. A Good Poultry Housing System Must Have Effective Waste Disposal Unit

In order to reduce or eliminate the outbreak of flu in your poultry, you must have an effective waste disposal unit. The truth is that in a poultry farm, you cannot rule out the death of some birds, but it is very important not to allow dead birds to liter all around your poultry farm. Beside the foul smell it will generate, it will also result to flu for both humans and your birds. Of course you know that waste from birds and bad eggs also generate offensive odor; so an effective waste disposal unit must be put in place.

i. A Good Poultry Housing System Must Have Different Steps (Confinements) for Different Ages and Species of Birds

It will be wrong to house birds of different ages and species in the same confinement. Some older birds can kill your chicks by stepping or perking them. So if you are considering raising different species of birds in your poultry farm, it is important that you build different confinements for them.

j. A Good Poultry System Must Have a Standard Hatchery Unit

A good poultry system must have a standard hatchery unit. It is economical to hatch your own eggs in your poultry as against going out to buy day old chicks. The truth is that, you will eliminate death of chicks in the process of transporting them when you have your own egg incubator within your poultry farm. You can decide to buy your own egg incubator or design it to meet your own specification. You might want to ask if these tips will help, you sure bet it will if you are careful to adhere to the tips listed above.

There you have it; the 10 tips and requirement for a good poultry housing system. Lets now learn how to house our flock.

The Housing of Hens

Modern domestic strains of hens come from Jungle Fowl and we know that in the wild, hens would build a nest for their egg, forage for food and perch at night. While modern strains of hen are different from their ancestors, they still retain many of the behavior patterns of their ancestors and are strongly motivated to perform those behaviors. The various types of housing systems used to raise egg-laying hen's on-farm are listed below.

The method of housing strongly impacts a bird's ability to perform natural behaviors and therefore impacts on their welfare. When we consider the various methods of housing, it can be useful to evaluate them in the context of what we know to be the natural behaviors of egg-laying hens.

Cage Systems

1. Conventional Battery Cages

These systems house egg-laying hens in small barren cages. These housing systems provide access to feed and water and droppings fall through the wire cage floor onto a belt or into a pit for disposal. The space provided for each hen varies across farms but generally 3 or more birds are housed in each cage and cages are stacked on top of each other.

Access to food and water is good and consistent in these systems with automated units providing adequate food and water for the birds throughout the laying cycle. Thermal comfort: Barn temperatures can be well-maintained so that birds are in an environment that consistently has appropriate temperatures. Physical comfort: There is broad consensus that the physical comfort of birds in conventional battery cages poor. For example, hens can experience chronic pain associated with injuries to their feet caused by standing on the wire floor of the cages. Another source of pain may come at the time of catching, and transport studies show that hens in battery cages have weak bones, due to lack of movement and are therefore more susceptible to bone fractures at catching and during transport.

Emotional well-being: Birds in battery cages are less likely to experience fear because they are in a small stable group of hens and predation is not an issue. However, much research suggests that hens in conventional cages experience severe frustration due to their confinement in these barren environments and their inability to nest while laying an egg. When we observe modern strains of hens around the time of egg-laying, we see behaviors symptomatic of frustration, including pacing and increased aggression. Ability to perform natural behaviors: These cages severely restrict freedom of movement the cages are barren and too small to allow the hens to perform important movements they are strongly motivated to perform, including grooming, wing flapping, perching and nest building.

2. Enriched/Modified/Furnished Cages

These systems are diverse in their design and may provide:

☐   More space per hen than a conventional battery cage

☐   Resources that enable hens to perform natural behaviors (e.g. nesting and perching)

Access to food and water

Is good and consistent in enriched cages. It is recommended that feed be provided in ground form rather than pelleted form, in order to encourage food-directed pecking behavior and to decrease the likelihood of feather pecking.

Thermal comfort:

Barn temperatures can be maintained so that birds are in an environment that has appropriate temperatures throughout their laying cycle. Physical comfort: The enriched cage will still restrict a hen's ability to roam freely, but depending on the space provided per bird, they will be able to flap their wings and preen. If the flooring is litter rather than wire, the birds will not suffer from the pain associated with foot injuries. However, the litter must be properly maintained so that it doesn't cause skin problems, such as foot pad dermatitis.

Emotional well-being Variable

If the enriched cage contains sufficient nest boxes and a suitable nest building substrate the birds will be able to fulfill this behavior and will not feel frustrated at the time of egg-laying. Birds are less likely to experience fear in these enriched cages because they are in a smaller stable group of hens and will not be fearful of predation. Ability to perform natural behaviors: Variable. If the enriched cage has a perch and dust bathing area, the hens will be able to perform those behaviors provided also that there is adequate space and adequate resources so that dominant birds do not guard the resources preventing others in the group from accessing them. Therefore, if you are looking to buy cages for your flock, i will advice you purchase an Enriched/Modified/Furnished Cages

Affordable Chicken Layer Cages for Sale in Nigeria

Find top quality and affordable layer cages for sale in Nigeria.

Chicken layer cages are generally used in the layer houses since they offer very easy management for many Nigerian poultry farmers who would like to upgrade the farming and make a little more intensive.

Many Nigerians increasingly prefer the chicken layer cages in Nigeria due to their many numerous advantages such as ease of management of the hens along with the ease of management of the eggs laid.

Above is a 128 capacity chicken cage for sale in Nigeria which comes with full accessories and fixtures along with 1 year warranty For smaller chicken house or smaller number of chickens, you can simply use a two-tier layer cage. Two tiers are stacked up to two levels. You should transfer the layers during the second laying cycle. Layers are generally kept in two laying cycles. The first cycle is the rearing cycle when you put them on chick and growers mash. This is generally the period from 0-20 weeks.

Chicken Cages in Nigeria offer you efficient management, less labor, less diseases and more productivity the second part refers to week 21 to week 60 when the hens begin laying eggs. This is usually a period of 40 weeks or 10 months. This is the period when you should introduce the hens into the layer cages. The price of the chicken cages in Nigeria depends on your capacity and the installation cost.

Prices of the chicken cages in Nigeria can start from as low as N35,000 for a chicken cage with a capacity of 128 chickens. The cages are made of the starter parts and the follower parts. The starter parts have the medication tanks and they supply fresh and clean drinking water to the rest of layer cages as well as the follower parts or sections of the cage.

Farmers can add as many follower sections as they wish based on their capacity or number of layers that they wish to add to the cages simultaneously. What will limit the length of the follower cages is really the length of the house.

Layer cages are built with a nipple drinking system which comes as part of the cage. The nipple drinker is installed above the chicken and allows them to get water by pecking at the nipple.

There is a trough that runs along the length of the chicken cage in order to make it easy to feed the chickens.

Specifications of the Layer cages

☐   They are made of galvanized steel

☐   They have nipple drinking systems accessories

☐   Built with medication tanks to make it easier to give medicine to all the chickens in the cages

☐   Have flexible troughs for feeding

Cage-Free Systems

1. Free Run

Hens are raised free from battery cages and are kept entirely indoors on a barn floor. Free run housing that provides deep-bedded sawdust (or other fibrous bedding material) is often referred to as a deep-litter system. Free run housing does not necessarily provide more space per hen than conventional battery cages, and is not required to provide resources such as nest boxes, perches, or a substrate for dust bathing.

While free run hens have no access to the outdoors, the barns may be designed to allow natural light to enter.

NOTE: The "free run" label that may be seen on some broiler (meat) chicken can mislead consumers by suggesting that meat chickens are raised in cages. In fact, no meat chickens are raised in cages; they are either free run or free range.

Access to food and water: Is good and consistent in these systems as long as a sufficient access is provided in each cage. It is recommended that feed be provided in ground form rather than pelleted form, in order to encourage food-directed pecking behaviour and to decrease the likelihood of feather-pecking.

Thermal comfort: Barn temperatures can be maintained so that birds are in an environment that has appropriate temperatures throughout their laying cycle. Physical comfort: Variable, depending on the space provided per bird. If the litter is well maintained, painful foot injuries will not be a problem. Emotional well-being: As the birds in a flock establish their hierarchy, some may be aggressive which may cause fearfulness in some birds; therefore it is important to provide the hens with escape areas.

Ability to perform natural behaviours: Well-managed free run facilities with appropriate stocking densities allow the hens to roam freely in the barn and explore their surroundings. If these systems provide nest boxes, perches and dust bathing areas in sufficient quantity, the hens in the flock will be able to fulfill their full range of natural behaviours. Studies show that birds who use perches regularly have stronger bones and are therefore less likely to suffer from painful injuries common in their battery-caged counterparts.

2. Free Range

Hens are free from battery cages and are allowed access to the outside. As with free-run housing, free-range systems do not necessarily provide more space than conventional battery cages, and are not required to provide resources such as nest boxes, perches, or a substrate for dust-bathing.

Access to food and water: Adequate feeders and drinkers must be available to the flock to ensure that all birds have good access. It is recommended that feed be provided in ground form rather than pelleted form, in order to encourage food-directed pecking behavior and to decrease the likelihood of feather pecking.

Thermal comfort: Will be variable in these systems; however, since hens can choose whether to be indoors or outdoors, their thermal comfort will likely be good. Flocks with access to the outdoors also require shade during the summer as well as shelter from rain.

Physical comfort: Variable depending on the space provided per bird, as per "free run" above. Emotional well-being: As the birds in a flock establish their hierarchy, some may be aggressive which may cause fearfulness in some birds and providing escape areas will help alleviate that. Any flock with access to the outside must be protected from external threats such as predators.

Ability to perform natural behaviors: As with "free run" above. Access to the outside also gives the birds the opportunity to forage for food as they like.

Chapter 11

Feeding Your Poultry

How do you feed your hens?

There is no magic to feeding chickens. Small flock producers can choose from many brands of feed produced by several manufacturers. These manufactured feeds are computer formulated by company nutritionists to provide optimal nutrition for the particular type and age of chicken being fed.

The formulation of these feeds, which is similar to commercial feeds, is based on years of research on commercial chickens. They are considered a complete diet, containing all of the nutrients required by chickens. In most cases, supplemental vitamins are unnecessary if these feeds are fed exclusively.

Feeds are formulated and manufactured for chickens to meet their nutritional needs at specific ages and production characteristics. For example, starter feeds are fed to chicks from hatch to a few weeks of age. Grower and developer feeds are fed to "adolescent" growing chickens, while layer or breeder feeds are fed to chickens that are producing eggs.

The ingredients in these different types of feeds are similar; however, the proportions vary to provide the proper level of nutrition for the particular birds being fed. Each sack is labeled with its specific use.

It is important to feed egg producing chickens the appropriate feed from hatch through their productive years to maximize their productivity. Feeding improperly at any stage can result in poor egg production. Whether they are bantams or large fowl, white or brown egg layers, all chickens' requirements for protein, carbohydrates, fats, fiber, vitamins, and minerals are similar.

Your birds rely on you to provide them with proper feed. If you do, they will produce many high quality eggs for the family and customers. Following a few simple feeding rules can lead to a healthy and productive flock.

Commercially raised layers hens receive three diets during the growing phase: **starter**, **grower**, and **developer/layers mash**. Most feed stores sell only one or two types of feeds for raising replacement pullets.

FEED	PROTEIN LEVEL (%)	AGE OF BIRDS	FEED INTAKE/10 BIRDS/ AGE PERIOD
Chick starter	18-20	0-6 weeks	20-29 lbs
Pullet grower	14-16	6-20 weeks	120-130 lbs
Layers mash	15-18	20 weeks on	18-24 lbs/week
All purpose*	16	All ages	

* Feed if only a single feed is available, and use during the entire growing period.

Starter feeds

Feed newly hatched chicks a starter diet until they are about 6 weeks old. Starter diets are formulated to give proper nutrition to fast growing baby chickens. These feeds usually contain between 18 and 20 percent protein.

It is not necessary to feed "meat bird starter" to young layer chickens. Diets formulated for starting meat chickens are higher in protein (22 percent) to maximize growth, which is not necessary or desirable for egg laying chickens and is higher in cost.

Grower and developer feeds

Once the birds reach about 6 weeks of age, substitute a grower feed for the starter. Grower feeds are about 15 or 16 percent protein and are formulated to sustain good growth to maturity. After about 14 weeks of age, you can substitute the grower feed with developer feeds if they are available. These feeds are lower in protein than grower feeds (14 to 15 percent) and are formulated to prepare young chickens for egg production.

Note: These two feed types are virtually interchangeable; either one can be fed to chickens between 6 weeks of age and the beginning of egg production.

Layer and breeder feeds

Once your chickens begin laying eggs, you can choose between layer and breeder feeds. Your choice of feed at this stage depends on how the eggs will be used.

Layer feeds are formulated for chickens that are laying table eggs (those used for food). Layer feeds contain about 16 percent protein and extra calcium so that the chickens will lay eggs with strong shells. Start feeding layer feeds at about 20 weeks of age or when the first egg is laid, whichever occurs first. Breeder feeds are formulated for chickens that are producing eggs for hatching. These feeds basically are layer feeds containing slightly more protein and fortified with extra vitamins for proper chick development and hatching.

However, use of breeder feeds is somewhat questionable for the small flock producer, since the increased cost may not be justified by the potentially slight increase in hatchability. You also may give both laying and breeding chickens access to ground oyster shell. Some high-producing laying birds may require the extra calcium provided by oyster shell, even though the prepared diet is a complete feed. The need to feed oyster shell can be determined by shell quality.

If eggs are laid with thin shells that are easily cracked or shells that are rough with almost a sandpaper feel, oyster shell may help to increase shell strength and quality. When feeding oyster shell, provide a separate feeder allowing free choice feeding on oyster shell.

Medicated feeds

Most commercial starter diets are medicated to prevent common yet serious diseases in chicken flocks. Medications are less common in grower or layer diets. Feeds that contain medications are labeled as such. Check the label for warnings concerning the medication used in feeds. Withdrawal dates will be indicated on the label if there is a risk of the medication's presence in the eggs. Feed medications are highly researched and regulated, so you can be confident that the eggs are safe to eat if you follow the label instructions.

If you wish to use non medicated feeds, they usually are available or can be ordered. However, in some cases, mortality levels, especially in young chicks, may rise to unacceptable levels if non medicated feeds are fed.

Water

Water is the single most important nutrient that chickens consume. Therefore, it is necessary to provide adequate amounts of clean, fresh water daily during growth and egg production. Chickens will drink between two and three times as much water by weight as they eat in feed. Their consumption of water increases in warm weather.

Scratch (grains)

Chickens love to scratch. They use their feet to disturb the litter or ground to find various seeds, greens, grit, or insects to eat. Feeding scratch grains can promote this behavior, which gives the birds exercise and keeps them busy. However, feeding scratch to chickens is not necessary when they are receiving a complete diet. Scratch feeds usually are cracked, rolled, or whole grains such as corn, barley, oats, or wheat, which are relatively low in protein and high in energy or fiber depending on which grains are used. When fed in concert with prepared feeds, they dilute nutrient levels in the carefully formulated diets. Therefore, you should provide scratch sparingly. A general rule of thumb is to feed only as much scratch as the chickens can consume in about 20 minutes, or about 10 to 15 percent of their total daily food consumption.

When feeding scratch, also provide an insoluble grit so that the birds can grind and digest the grains properly. If the birds have access to the ground they usually can find enough grit in the form of small rocks or pebbles.

Otherwise, you can purchase grit. Oyster shell cannot be substituted for grit because it is too soft to aid in grinding.

Table scraps and greens

Chickens, like other family pets, enjoy many of the same foods their owners do. However, excessive feeding of table scraps and greens may not be beneficial to the birds or to their productivity. Some supplementation is fine; in fact, greens help to keep egg yolks deep yellow in color but, as with scratch, these foods should be limited. The same rule applies here: the total supplementation of scratch and table scraps should be no more than can be cleaned up in about 20 minutes.

Feeding management

The mechanics of feeding are nearly as important as the feed itself. Supply enough feeder space so that all the birds can eat at the same time. When space is limited, some birds don't get enough to eat. Keep feed available for the birds constantly (ad libitum). Meal feeding (giving a limited amount of feed several times each day) can reduce productivity if not managed carefully.

Place feeders and drinkers so that the trough is at the level of the birds' backs. This practice reduces feed spillage, which encourages rodents, wastes feed, and costs money. If bantams and large fowl are feeding and drinking from the same equipment, adjust it to the bantams.

Store feed for a maximum of 2 months, and keep it in a cool, dry place. Some molds that grow in damp feeds are dangerous for chickens, and old feeds can lose some of their nutritional value.

The A-Z of making your own quality chicken feed at home to cut costs

Making own chiken feeds

In Summary

❖ Poor quality feeds lead to a slow growth in chickens, low egg production, diseases or even death.

❖ Making poultry feeds on the farm is one of the best ways to maintain quality.

Except for a few feed manufacturers who keep to the standards in poultry feed formulations, many feed companies in the country make very poor quality feeds, a situation which has led huge losses. Poor quality feeds lead to a slow growth in chickens, low egg production, diseases or even death. Making poultry feeds on the farm is one of the best ways to maintain quality and cut the cost of production.

The common ingredients are whole maize, maize germ, cotton seed cake, soya beans, sunflower or fish meal (omena). In addition, farmers need to add several feed additives (micronutrients, minerals and vitamins) to make sure their chicken have a balanced feed that meets their daily nutrient requirements.

Material is cheaply, available especially after the harvesting season. Depending on the cost of raw material, farmers who make their own feeds at home save between 30 to 50 per cent for every 100kg bag of chicken feed, depending on the source of their raw materials. Due to government regulation, major feed companies have reduced the standard quantity of feed from 25kg per bag, but the price of feed still remains almost the same. This means that farmers who are able to make their own feed make great savings on feeds which take up to 70 per cent of the production costs.

To formulate feeds, farmers have to use the Pearson Square method. In this method, the digestible crude protein (DCP) is the basic nutritional requirement for any feed preparation for all animals and birds.

Now, assuming that a farmer wants to make feed for their chicken using this method, they have to know the crude protein content of each of the ingredients they want to use to make their feed.

The following are the DCP values for each of the common ingredients used in feed making:

Whole maize ...8.23%

Soya been cake... 45%

Fishmeal (omena)...55%

Maize bran...........7%

Sunflower............35%

Each category of chicken has its nutritional requirement. For example, if we want to make feed for layers, the feed should have at least 18 per cent crude protein. If one is to formulate feed for layers, then they would have to calculate the percentage of DCP in each of the ingredients they want to use to ensure that the total crude protein content is at least 18 per cent.

Therefore, to make a 70kg bag of feed for layers, a farmer would require the following ingredients:

34kg of whole maize

12kg of soya

8kg of omena (fishmeal)

10kg of maize bran

6kg of lime (as a calcium source)

To find out if all the above ingredients meet this standard of 18% crude protein, a farmer can do a simple calculation as follows:

Whole maize — 34kg x 8.23 ÷100 = 2.80 %

Soya — 12kg x 45kg ÷ 100 = 5.40 %

Omena — 8 kg x 55kg ÷ 100 = 4.40 %

Lime — 6 kg x 0 kg ÷ 100 = 0.00%

Total % of crude protein = 13.30%

To get the total crude protein percentage of all these ingredients in a 70kg bag of feed, the farmer should take this crude protein content of the combined ingredients, divide by 70kg and multiply by 100, thus; 13.30 ÷70 ×100 = 19%; this shows that the crude protein content of the above feed formulation is 19%, which is quite adequate for layers. You can still use same formula to calculate the feed for 100kg.

To ensure the chicken to get all they need in terms of nutrients such as vitamins, minerals and amino acids, you need these additives in their standard quantities.

In order to make it even simpler for farmers who would wish to make their own feeds, below are feed formulations for each category of chickens and stage of growth already worked out such that all the farmer needs is to buy the ingredients and mix them:

Making a 70 kg layers of layers chick mash (1-4 weeks)

Growing chicks require feed with Digestible Crude Protein (DCP) of between 18 to 20 per cent. The following formulation can be used to make a 70kg bag of layers chick mash:

Ingredients

31.5kg of whole maize

9.1kg of wheat bran

7.0kg of wheat pollard

16.8 kg of sunflower (or 16.8 kg of linseed)

1.5kg of fishmeal

1.75kg of lime

30g of salt

20g of premix Amino acids

70g of tryptophan

3.0g of lysine

10g of methionine

70 g of Threonine

50g of enzymes

60g of coccidiostat

50g of toxin binder

Making a 70 kg bag of growers mash (4 to 8 weeks)

Growers (pullets or young layers) should be provided with feed having a protein content of between 16 and 18 per cent. Such feed makes the young layers to grow fast in preparation for egg laying:

10kg of whole maize

17kg of maize germ

13kg of wheat pollard

10kg of wheat bran

6kg of cotton seed cake

5kg of sunflower cake

3.4kg of soya meal

2.07kg of lime

700g of bone meal

3kg of fishmeal

Additives

14g of salt

1g of coccidiostat

18g of Pre-mix

1g of zinc bacitracitrach

7g of mycotoxin binder

Making a 70 kg bag of layers' mash (18 weeks and above)

Ingredients

34kg of whole maize

12kg of Soya

8kg of fishmeal

10kg of maize bran, rice germ or wheat bran

6kg of lime

Amino acids

175g premix

70g lysine

35g methionine

70kg Threonine

35g tryptophan

50g toxin binder

Layer feed should contain a Digestible Crude Protein (DCP) content of between 16-18 per cent.

The feed should contain calcium (lime) for the formation of eggshells (laying hens that do not get enough calcium will use the calcium stored in their own born tissue to produce eggshells).

Layer feed should be introduced at 18 weeks.

If you would like also to learn about broilers feed formulation, below is the procedure:

Formulating a 70 kg bag of broiler feed

Broilers have different feed requirements in terms of energy, proteins and minerals during different stages of their growth. It is important that farmers adapt feed rations to these requirements for maximum production.

Young broilers have a high protein requirement for the development of muscles, feathers, etc. As the broilers grow, their energy requirements for the deposit of fat increase and their protein requirements decrease.

They therefore require high protein content in their starter rations than in the grower and finisher rations.

Broilers should have feed that has between 22 -24 per cent DCP. The following guidelines can help the farmer to make the right feed at each stage of growth:

Broiler starter feed (1-4 weeks)

40kg of whole maize

12kg of fishmeal (or omena)

14kg of soya bean meal

4kg of lime

70g of premix

Amino acids

35g of lysine

35g of Threonine

Preparing broiler Finisher feed (70kg)

10kg of whole maize

16.7kg of maize germ

13.3kg of wheat pollard

10 kg wheat bran

6 kg of cotton seed cake

4.7kg of sunflower cake

3kg of fishmeal 2kg of lime

3.4kg of soya meal

40g of bone meal

10g of grower PMX

5g of salt

5g of coccidiostat

5g of Zincbacitrach

Tested poultry feed formulae for maximum result

S. NO	Ingredients	Broiler starter	Broiler finisher
		MIXING PERCENTAGE	
1	Maize	62.25	67.75
2	Soya bean meal	34.00	29.00
3	Common salt	00.25	00.25
4	D.C.P	02.00	02.00
5	Vit. Premix	00.15	00.15
6	Trace minerals	00.15	00.15
7	Lime stone	01.20	01.20
	Total	**100.00**	**100.00**

Chick Ration		
Ingredients	**% compositions**	
1	maize	30
2	Wheat	20
3	Wheat bran	10
4	Rice bran	10
5	Sunflower/ GNC	10
6	Cotton seed	5
7	Fish meal	2
8	Beans	10
9	Bone meal	1
10	Lime stone	0.5
11	Salt	0.5
12	Mineral premix	1
	TOTAL	**100**

S.N	Ingredients	Starter phase (%)	Finisher phase (%)
1	Maize	46.00	50.00
2.	Soybean meal	18.50	12.00
3	Groundnut cake	15.00	11.00
4	Fish meal	2.00	2.00
5	Wheat offal	12.45	19.05
6	Bone meal	2.00	2.00
7	Oyster shell	3.00	3.00
8	Salt	0.25	0.25
9	Premix	0.25	0.25
10	methionine	0.30	0.25
11	lysine	0.25	0.20
12		100	100

Calculated:

Crude protein

	Starter	Finisher
ME (MJ/Kg)	23.05	19.91
Ether extract (%)	11.73	11.71
Crude fibre (%)	3.93	3.89
Calcium (%)	3.67	3.79
Phosphorus (%)	1.75	1.74

	0.43	0.41

NOTE: For farmers who have more than 500 chickens, it is advisable to make 1 ton of feed at once (There are 14 bags of feed in one ton of 70kg bags).

Therefore, to make 1 ton of feed, all a farmer needs is to multiply each of the Ingredients by 14. Ensure that all the feed you make will last for one month and not longer — this ensures the feed remains fresh and safe for chickens. Any feed that lasts more than one month may deteriorate in quality and can affect your chickens.

Daily feed requirements for each growth stage

Farmers should maintain the right feed quantities for chicken at each stage of growth as shown below:

❖   An egg-laying chicken requires 130-140g of feed per day.

❖   A chick requires a minimum 60g per day. If they finish their daily rations, give them fruit and vegetable cuttings to ensure they feed continuously.

❖ Young chickens (or pullets) which are about to start laying eggs should be fed 60g for 2 and ½ months and then put on layer diet (140g per day). Supplement the feed with vegetables, edible plant leaves and fruit peelings in addition to their feed rations.

❖ Broiler chicks require 67g per day. Broiler finishers require 67g of feed per day to the day of slaughter.

☐ Chickens are very sensitive to aflotoxins - never use rotten maize while making feeds.

Where to buy ingredients

Farmers who need raw materials for feed making including feed additives (pre-mixes and amino acids) can order them from agro veterinary shops nearest to them. There are also companies doing calibration services for farmers who wish to make feeds in large scale farming enterprises and even for any farmer who requires these services.

Important tips on feed preparation

When making home-made feed rations, it is important to do experimental trials, by isolating a number of chickens, feeding them and observing their performance. If the feed rations are right, the broilers will grow fast and layers will increase egg production (at least 1 egg after every 27 hours).

Buy quality fishmeal from reputable companies. If omena is used, the farmers must be sure of its quality; most of the omena in the open-air markets may be contaminated. Farmers are advised to go for soya meal if they cannot get good quality omena.

Always mix the micronutrients (amino acids) first before mixing them with the rest of the feed.

For mixing, farmers are advised to use a drum mixer. Never use a shovel to mix feed because the ingredients will be unevenly distributed.

Important: To improve on the feed quality, farmers making their own feeds should always have it tested to ensure the feed is well balanced.

All the above feed formula has been tested in the laboratory. Farmers producing their own feed in large quantity need not to use trial and error method rather use modern feed testing equipment that can test all nutrients and even the quality of the raw material used. It costs N1, 000 to test one sample.

After preparing your feed, take a 1kg sample; send it by courier to any food laboratory centre in your region. If you are on email, the centre can send the results to you within 24 hours.

Chapter 12

Health Management

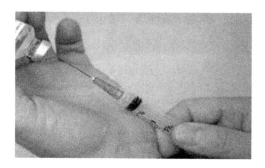

Vaccination

The demand for vaccination of layers flock has increased with the popularity of keeping chickens.

Why should we vaccinate?

Vaccination is commonly used in commercial poultry and increasingly in backyard birds to control disease. Vaccines mimic natural infection, allowing the birds to build up immunity to the disease without any of the harmful effects. This way you can prevent your birds getting the disease.

Are there any problems with vaccination?

No! Vaccine can be 100% effective, if the birds are vaccinated but exposed to large levels of the wild disease then the immunity generated by the vaccine can be overcome. Also many diseases, such as Infectious Bronchitis (IB), will have several strains so it may mean the strain your bird has been vaccinated against may not be the same as the disease strains in your area.

Many of the vaccines come in large doses for commercial flocks and therefore there is a lot of wastage for people with a small flock; however even with the waste it is still reasonably cheap to vaccinate.

It is very important to remember that the success of the vaccination depends on good vaccination technique. Vaccines are very vulnerable and are therefore easily destroyed.

What diseases can I vaccinate against?

There are a range of diseases which can be vaccinated against but below are some of the most common ones:

- ☐ Mareks Disease

- ☐ Infectious Bronchitis (IB)

- ☐ Avian RhinoTracheitis (ART)

- ☐ *Mycoplasma gallisepticum (MG)*

- ☐ *Salmonella*

Should I vaccinate?

The need to vaccinate, and which disease you should vaccinate against will depend on your holding, the number of birds you are keeping and whether or not you buy in or sell out birds.

VACCINATION PROGRAMME FOR HENS The programme below must serve as a guideline.

Age	Disease	Vaccination route
1 day	Marek's Disease (HVT/SB1 or HVT/Rispens)	Injection
18 days	Infectious Bursal Disease	Drinking water
24 days	Infectious Bursal Disease Newcastle Bronchitis	Drinking water Drinking water Drinking water
30 days	Infectious Bursal Disease	Drinking water
6 weeks	Newcastle Bronchitis	Spray Spray
10 weeks	Avian Encephalomyelitis[2] Newcastle Bronchitis	Spray Spray Spray
13 weeks	Avian Encephalomyelitis[2] Pox Newcastle Bronchitis Salmonella	Wing-web Wing-web Injection Injection Injection
15 weeks	Newcastle Bronchitis	Spray Spray

Drugs / vaccine Administration schedule in Broiler birds			
S.N	WINDOW DAYS	MEDICATION/ VACCINE TYPE	ROUTE

1	1 – Day 5	Glucos/NDV/ Lasota (1st shot)	i/o oral
2	6 - 7	Vitamins /antibiotics	oral
3	8 - 10	Anticoccidiosis	oral
4	12 – 13	IBD Gumboro (1st shot)	oral
5	Day 14	Vitamins	oral
6	Day 21	NDV/ Lasota (2ndt shot)	oral
7	22 - 24	Vitamins	oral
8	25 - 26	Anticoccidiosis	oral
9	28 -30	IBD Gumboro (2nd shot)	oral
10	31 - 33	Vitamins	oral
11	34 -40	CRD Vaccine/drugs	oral
12	45 - 50	Vitamins	oral
13	52 – 60	Clean water, no medication	oral

Note. All medications should be withdrawn at least 8 days to sale or slaughter.

With regard to Mareks disease, in general, I recommend against vaccination unless there is a problem on the site. The vaccine is given to day old chicks as an injection into their breast, thigh or the back of the neck. But remember that day old chicks are small and fragile and can easily be injured by an inexperienced vaccinator. Incorrect vaccination with a needle can cause excessive damage to the chicks or even death.

The three respiratory diseases (IB/ MG/ ART) can all be vaccinated against. If you have respiratory disease on your holding it is probably worth getting a blood test carried out to ascertain which of these diseases are involved to ensure you are vaccinating against the correct ones. In general, if you are buying or selling a lot of birds it is worth considering vaccinating against all three. The vaccination consists of giving your birds two injections four weeks apart followed by an annual booster.

Salmonella vaccination consists of giving your birds two injections four weeks apart followed by an annual booster. However it is important to note that the vaccination only protects your birds against *S. Enteritidis* and *S. Typhimurium* and as such your birds have the potential to pick up other *Salmonella* species.

In conclusion, you can vaccinate against a number of diseases and which ones you should vaccinate against will depend on your individual holding, how many birds you have, if you buying/selling a lot of birds and which diseases have been found on your holding in the past. Please remember vaccination is not without its problems and it is not 100% effective.

If you are considering and you are a beginner in raising layers poultry vaccination please contact a Chicken Vet for advice on vaccinations.

Vaccination Advice

- ❖ do not add vaccine to chlorinated water without using a protective dyes

- ❖ make sure the area where you make up the vaccine is clean

- ❖ do not contaminate the vaccine with disinfectants

- ❖ do not withdraw the water for too long

- ❖ make sure the birds all have vaccine added water at the same time

- ❖ Make sure you wash and dry the drinkers very well before using to give water soluble vaccines

- ❖ Make sure the vaccine is in a good state and within the recommended temperature and if possibly give the vaccine with cool water

- ❖ Do not allow the vaccine stay longer after giving to the birds; remove the remaining water in less than 30 minutes of administration.

- ❖ Do not dilute the vaccine under a sun shine, in fact diluted inside a dark room.

- ❖ Do not all the birds spill the vaccine water on the floor of the pen to avoid infection

Vaccines by injection

The most common times to give a vaccine by injection is at day old for Mareks disease or at point of lay to ensure a good level of protection during lay against Infectious Bronchitis, Turkey Rhiontracheitis Virus, Newcastle Disease, Egg Drop Syndrome and possibly *Mycoplasma gallisepticum*.

Ensure you learn how to vaccinate birds by injection as there are many problems and possible welfare issues if the technique, which is not difficult, is not carried out correctly.

Common Diseases in Hens

A variety of diseases affect poultry of all kinds, ages and sexes. But certain ailments primarily strike laying hens. These diseases cause reproductive issues and can kill your bird. Practicing good preventive measures can reduce the chances of your hens becoming ill. These include quarantining new hens for at least three weeks before introducing them to your flock.

How to know that your Hens are sick

Signs of Infection include

- ☐ Unthriftiness
- ☐ Lack of appetite and sneezing
- ☐ Dullness
- ☐ Persistent coughing
- ☐ Rough coat
- ☐ Watery, foul smelling or blood stained faces,
- ☐ Ruffled feathers
- ☐ Discharge of mucus from the nostrils,
- ☐ Anus or vents (in birds) may be pasted with stool
- ☐ Reduced production
- ☐ Reduced weight
- ☐ Reduced water intake
- ☐ Decreased activity and movement

☐ Discharge from the mouth and eyes

☐ Drooping tongue

☐ Impaired vision

☐ Abnormal body temperature

☐ Distension of abdominal contents

☐ Morality rate increases

☐ Mortality rate increases

☐ There could be abortion threat.

Signs of Good Health in Animals

Sign, contrary to those given, may indicate ill-health. The main signs of good health in animals are:

❖ Good appetite

❖ Eating with relish and coddling in ruminants.

❖ Bright eyes and pink membrane

❖ Normal temperature, and pulse

❖ Normal breathing rate

❖ Moist nostrils which are free of discharge.

❖ Normal faeces

❖ Soft, smooth and tender skin

❖ Gain in weight in growing animals

❖ Increase egg production

❖ Clear coloured urine

❖ Increased quantity and quality of milk production

❖ No discharge around the anus and vulva of female animals.

SPREAD OF DISEASE

A disease can spread rapidly among chickens because they are usually kept together in a cage or chicken house. They also share the same food and waterfowls, which can spread disease and infections from sick to healthy chickens.

In an intensive system we place a great deal of pressure on the chickens to grow fast and to lay many eggs. This situation can cause disease to spread resulting in a lot of damage because of the stress the chicken's experience

FACTORS CONTRIBUTING TO DISEASE

Factors that can contribute to disease include management, environment and the chickens themselves

Management

☐ Poor-quality food and water

☐ Poor hygiene and inadequate cleaning programme

☐ Leaking water bowls

☐ Rat and fly problems

☐ Overcrowding of chicks

☐   Chickens of mixed ages reared together

☐   No security measures to prevent people and animals from entering the chicken house

Environment

☐   Too hot or too cold conditions

☐   Wet litter

☐   Dusty bedding

☐   High build up of chicken droppings

☐   No air circulation

☐   Sharp wires in the cages

Chickens

☐   Young chickens

☐   Weak second-grade chickens

☐   Chickens affected with other diseases

☐   Poor condition as a result of underfeeding

☐   No vaccination

ACTIONS AT FIRST SIGNS OF DISEASE

You must act quickly at the first signs of disease. The chickens must be treated, and management that may have led to the problem must be corrected to prevent the disease from occurring again

❖ Consult your animal health technician or veterinarian to help you find a correct solution to your problem as soon as possible

❖ Call your animal health technician or veterinarian. They will kill some of the sick chickens and cut them open. They will also cut open dead chickens and take samples. They may take blood or egg samples, depending on the disease. The samples taken will be sent to a laboratory.

❖ You and your animal health technician or veterinarian should then go through the entire system to identify possible problems in the management and environment that can be corrected

GENERAL TREATMENT

❖ There are not many forms of treatment or in certain cases no treatment for some diseases, which is why prevention is so important

❖ The treatment will depend on the cause of the disease
❖ If it is at all possible, try to separate all sick chickens from the healthy ones daily. The sick chickens should be handled and treated last to prevent the spread of the disease

❖ Correct management problems

GENERAL PREVENTION

Diseases can be prevented through management, environmental and chicken factors;

Management

☐   Apply correct methods for raising young chicks (temperature, food, water, bedding)

☐   Disinfect and clean the housing of the different groups of chicks

☐   Maintain the correct stocking density (avoid over-crowding)

☐   Use the best-quality food that is available and provide clean water daily

☐   Use bedding that is not dusty

☐   Prevent the buildup of gases by cleaning and ventilation

☐   Control rats and flies

☐   Ensure that no people from outside your farm visit the chicken house

☐ Have bird-proof houses to keep out wild birds that eat the food and bring diseases to your chickens

Environment

☐ Ensure that the building or house you are going to use is large enough for the chickens

☐ Fix leaky water troughs

☐ Feed and water bowls should be cleaned daily and fresh food and water should be supplied

☐ Dust causes irritation of the respiratory tract and the environment must therefore not be dusty

☐ Use cages for laying hens that do not have sharp edges that can injure the hens.

☐ Make sure that there is sufficient space per hen

Chickens

☐   Get only first-grade chicks from a good and reliable supplier

☐   Vaccinate chicks against important diseases

☐   Keep chickens of the same age together in one house

Types of disease

There are four main **types of disease** affecting poultry: metabolic and nutritional diseases; infectious diseases; parasitic diseases; and behavioral diseases.

1. Metabolic and nutritional diseases

These are conditions caused by a disturbance of normal metabolic functions either through a genetic defect, inadequate or inappropriate nutrition or impaired nutrient utilization. These include Fatty Liver Syndrome, Perosis (or slipped tendon), Rickets and Cage Layer Fatigue.

2. Infectious diseases

An infectious disease is any disease caused by invasion of a host by a pathogen which subsequently grows and multiplies in the body. Infectious diseases are often contagious, which means they can be spread directly or indirectly from one living thing to another.

These include Avian Encephalomyelitis, Avian Influenza, Avian Tuberculosis, Chicken Anaemia Virus Infection (or CAV), Chlamydiosis, Egg Drop Syndrome (or EDS), Fowl Cholera (or Pasteurellosis), Fowl Pox, Infectious Bronchitis, Infectious Bursal Disease (or Gumboro), Infectious Coryza, Infectious Laryngotracheitis, Lymphoid Leukosis, Marek's Disease, Mycoplasmosis, Necrotic Enteritis, Newcastle Disease and Salmonellosis.

3. Parasitic diseases

Parasitic diseases are infections or infestations with parasitic organisms. They are often contracted through contact with an intermediate vector, but may occur as the result of direct exposure. A parasite is an organism that lives in or on, and takes its nourishment from, another organism. A parasite cannot live independently. These include Coccidiosis, Cryptosporidiosis, Histomoniasis, Lice and Mites, Parasitic Worms (or Helminths), Toxoplasmosis and Trichomoniasis.

4. Behavioral diseases

Abnormal behavioral patterns can lead to injury or ill health of the abnormally behaving bird and/or its companions. These include Cannibalism (or aggressive pecking).

List of avian diseases

Poultry can be affected by many types of disease and a wide variety of pests (and behavioral problems) including those in the list below.

Diseases caused by Viruses

☐   Avian Influenza

☐   Avian Encephalomyelitis

☐   Big Liver and Spleen Disease

☐   Chicken Anaemia Virus Infection (or CAV)

☐   Egg drop syndrome (or EDS)

☐   Fowl Pox

☐   Inclusion Body Hepatitis (or Fowl adenovirus type 8)

☐   Infectious Bronchitis

☐   Infectious Bursal Disease (or Gumboro)

- [ ] Infectious Laryngotracheitis

- [ ] Leucosis

- [ ] Lymphoid Leukosis

- [ ] Lympoid Tumour Disease (Reticuloendotheliosis)

- [ ] Marek's Disease Virus or MDV

- [ ] Newcastle Disease

- [ ] Runting/stunting and malabsorption syndromes

- [ ] Viral Arthritis (Tenosynovitis)

Diseases caused by Chlamydia

- [ ] Chlamydiosis

Diseases caused by Mycoplasmas

☐   Mycoplasmosis – MG (Mycoplasma *gallisepticum*; MG infection; Chronic Respiratory Disease)

☐   Mycoplasmosis – MS (Mycoplasma *synoviae*; infectious synovitis)

Diseases caused by Bacteria

☐   Botulism

☐   Colibacillosis

☐   Infectious Coryza

☐   Fowl Cholera (or pasteurellosis)

☐   Necrotic Enteritis

☐   Paratyphoid

☐   Pullorum

☐   Spirochaetosis (Avian Intestinal Spirochaetosis)

☐ Tuberculosis (Avian Tuberculosis)

Diseases caused by Fungi

☐ Aspergillosis

☐ Favus

☐ Moniliasis (Candidiasis; crop mycosis)

Diseases caused by Protozoa

☐ Coccidiosis

☐ Cryptosporidiosis

☐ Histomoniasis

☐ Toxoplasmosis

☐ Trichomoniasis

Diseases caused by Internal Parasites

☐   Round worms

☐   Caecal worms

☐   Capillary worms

☐   Tape worms

Diseases caused by External Parasites

☐   Several types of louse (insect; plural – lice)

☐   Stick fast flea (insect)

☐   Fowl tick

☐   Several types of mite (acarid)

Diseases caused by Metabolic Disorders

☐   Ascites (waterbelly)

☐   Cage Layer Fatigue and Rickets

☐   Fatty Liver Haemorrhagic Syndrome

Diseases caused by environmental factors

☐   Cannibalism (or aggressive pecking)

☐   Caged Layer Fatigue

Pests

☐   Darkling Beetles

Lets now look at this diseases one by one;

Ascites

Ascites is considered a metabolic disorder and is common in commercially grown chicken and ducks. It is thought that in fast growing breeds, organs are unable to supply the body's cells with oxygen. The high oxygen requirement is a result of accelerated metabolic rates.

Avian encephalomyelitis

Avian encephalomyelitis (AE) is a viral infection of the central nervous system of poultry, primarily chickens, turkeys, Japanese (coturnix) quail, and pheasants. It is found worldwide and is characterised by ataxia (loss of muscle coordination) and tremors, especially of the head and neck, and a drop in egg production and hatchability in hens. Ducklings, pigeons, and guinea fowl can be infected experimentally. The mortality rate from this disease can be high.

The disease is most common in chickens 1-6 weeks of age. Symptoms usually appear at 7-10 days of age, although they may be present at hatching or delayed for several weeks. Affected chicks may first show a dull expression of the eyes, followed by unsteadiness, sitting on hocks, tremors of the head and neck, paresis (weakness or partial paralysis), and finally total paralysis. Feed and water consumption decreases and birds will lose weight. All stages of the disease can usually be seen in affected flocks. Muscle tremors are best seen after exercising the bird and head tremors are best seen by holding the bird inverted. In adult birds a slight transient drop in egg production may be the only symptom. The disease in turkeys is often milder than in chickens.

What causes avian encephalomyelitis?

AE is caused by a picornavirus. Vertical transmission is the most common way the disease is spread but it is also spread by direct contact between susceptible hatchlings and infected birds. Most commercial poultry are exposed in the hatchery when 1 day of age, although further spread occurs later within the flock. The virus present in droppings may survive for more than 4 weeks. Recovered birds are immune and do not spread the virus.

Prevention and treatment of avian encephalomyelitis

There is no treatment for AE. Control of the disease is through prevention. To prevent flocks becoming infected, hatcheries should only accept hatching eggs from immune breeder flocks. Lifetime immunity is acquired through vaccination or recovery from the disease. Breeder pullets should be vaccinated between 9-16 weeks of age. It is also recommended for replacement egg layer pullets to be vaccinated at this age to prevent a temporary drop in egg production.

To minimize the impact of the disease in an infected flock, remove all affected birds and provide good nursing, including fresh food and water, to the remaining birds. Affected birds should be killed and incinerated.

Avian influenza

Avian influenza (AI) is a highly contagious viral infection which may cause up to 100% mortality in chickens. The disease is caused by a virus that belongs to the family Orthomyxoviridae. Influenza viruses have two surface proteins, haemagglutinin and neuraminidase, that determine their subtype and the animal species they infect; there are 16 haemagglutinin and nine neuraminidase types.

When AI viruses of two haemagglutinin types, H5 and H7, infect poultry (chickens or turkeys) they often mutate and virulent disease arises in these birds which is called highly pathogenic avian influenza (HPAI). The initial infection that does not cause or causes minimal disease is called low pathogenic avian influenza (LPAI). Wild water birds act as reservoir hosts of influenza viruses; however these viruses generally do not cause disease in these birds.

Birds susceptible to AI

All commercial, domestic and wild bird species are susceptible to infection with AI viruses but disease outbreaks occur more frequently in chickens and turkeys. LPAI viruses are traditionally spread by migratory wild birds. Many species of waterfowl, especially geese, ducks and swans, carry the virus but generally show no signs of disease.

Spread of infection

Direct or indirect contact (likely through drinking water) with migratory waterfowl is the most likely source of infection for poultry. Once established in domestic poultry, infection can also spread through contact with contaminated equipment or humans. Transmission through the egg is uncommon, although contamination of the shell does occur. Avian influenza virus is highly concentrated in the manure and in nasal and eye discharges.

Prevention of infection

Develop bio-security plans to prevent avian influenza viruses gaining entry to commercial poultry flocks. The plans are aimed at limiting possible contact between wild birds and domestic poultry through contaminated water and food supplies and transfer of infection by the mechanical movement of infection on fomites such as on the clothing and footwear of persons and on equipment, containers, vehicles etc. Treatment of surface water by chlorination to inactivate the virus is essential if it is to be supplied to poultry and aviary birds.

Avian Intestinal Spirochaetosis

Avian Intestinal Spirochaetosis (AIS) is a disease that affects commercial laying and meat breeding hens and results from the colonisation of the caeca and rectum by one or more species of anaerobic spirochaetal bacteria. AIS were first described in the 1990s in commercial chickens from the United Kingdom, The Netherlands and the United States. Seven species of the bacterium are capable of colonising poultry hosts, but only three are considered to be pathogenic. Of these, *Brachyspira intermedia* is considered the most common and significant species.

AIS is characterized by chronic diarrhea in diseased birds, and subsequently results in faecal staining of eggs and wet litter. The resultant wet litter is an industrial problem and necessitates the mechanical cleaning of cages. A delay and (or) reduction of egg laying capacity is also observed, and hatched broiler chicks from eggs of infected parents show reduced performance compared to those of healthy parents. The significance of AIS is often unappreciated due to the variable clinical signs of the disease. In addition, the isolation of the bacterium can only be achieved using specialized media and techniques.

Treatment

Currently there are no antimicrobial compounds that are registered for treatment of, or vaccines for prevention of, AIS. Compounds that are used to treat or prevent spirochaetosis in pigs have also been used in laying chickens with limited success, and importantly have not provided any long term control with recurrence of infection and reduction in performance occurring within 3 weeks to 3 months.

Research is currently in progress to develop a diagnostic immunological test method and a recombinant vaccine to detect antibodies and provide sufficient protection against AIS in chickens.

Avian tuberculosis

Avian tuberculosis is chronic bacterial infection that spreads slowly through a flock. All bird species appear to be susceptible, however pheasants seem highly susceptible. The disease is more common in captive than wild birds; however it is uncommon in poultry flocks due to the poultry husbandry practices and their short life span.

Symptoms do not usually develop until late in the infection and affected hens are usually more than one year old. The disease in birds is characterized by gradual weight loss, sluggishness and sometimes lameness. Combs and wattles shrink and become pale.

The disease causes multiple granulomas (a small mass of firm tissue formed as a result of inflammation) to form in a number of organs, predominantly in the liver, spleen, intestine and bone marrow.

What causes avian tuberculosis?

Avian tuberculosis is caused by the bacterium *Mycobacterium avium*. This bacterium is closely related to the human and bovine TB bacteria. It can survive for as long as four years in the soil or when protected by organic matter. It is also resistant to acid and alkali. Infected birds with advanced granulomas excrete the bacteria in their faeces. Infected dead birds and offal may infect penmates, rodents and predators if eaten. The bacterium can spread from bird to bird, animal to bird and bird to animal. The incubation period is several weeks to months.

Prevention and treatment of avian tuberculosis

There is not treatment for avian tuberculosis. Control is achieved through depopulation and good bio-security practices including rodent control, screening against wild birds, isolation from other birds and animals and good sanitation. Dirt-floored houses should have several inches of the floor removed and replaced with dirt from a place where poultry have not been maintained.

Cannibalism (or aggressive pecking)

A victim of cannibalism

Pecking is the natural means by which poultry investigate their surroundings and establish a stable social order; however this behaviour can escalate to the stage where birds will literally peck each other to death (**cannibalism**). All forms of commercial poultry can experience cannibalism as it a behavioural problem that can develop into a habit that will persist and spread within a flock as a learned behaviour, even after the initial causes of the behaviour have been corrected.

What causes cannibalism?

Cannibalism often starts as feather pulling or picking while the birds are only a few weeks old, or as investigative pecking at any age. These behaviours can escalate to aggressive pecking, particularly if injury occurs. Scientific study has shown that any stressor (or combination of stressors) can trigger this behaviour and can lead to serious aggressive pecking and cannibalism.

These stressors include crowding, bright light intensity, high room temperature, poor ventilation, high humidity, low salt, trace nutrient deficiency, insufficient feeding or drinking space, nervous and excitable birds (hereditary), external parasites, access to sick or injured birds, stress from moving, boredom and idleness, housing birds of different appearance together and birds prolapsing during egg-laying.

Prevention and treatment of cannibalism

As cannibalism can become a learned behaviour it can be difficult to treat once it has started in a flock. Therefore prevention should be the main aim and as such, good husbandry practices should aim to minimize the stressors listed above as potential causes for cannibalism. Some strains of birds have been shown to have a higher tendency towards developing aggressive pecking behaviour and therefore strains that are more placid should be preferred.

The broad range of factors that can trigger cannibalism can make it very difficult for management to control all of these factors for the entire life of the flock. Bright light is a known factor that leads to cannibalism but control of lighting levels in some poultry housing systems can be very difficult, if not impossible (such as in free range systems). Where outbreaks of cannibalism have occurred in a flock, or where there is a reasonable concern that management strategies can not be guaranteed to prevent an outbreak, then beak trimming of the birds may be used as a control measure. Trimming of the sharp tip of the upper, and sometimes also lower, beak reduces the damage that is caused by aggressive pecking.

The spread of the behaviour may be able to be controlled if the injured and aggressive birds can be rapidly identified and removed from the flock. Provision of escape areas may also help in floor-housed flocks. Other control methods that have been tested include the use of spectacles to prevent forward vision, bits that prevent complete closure of the beak and coloured contact lenses to prevent the identification of blood on another bird.

There is evidence that cannibalism may be alleviated through the use of high fibre diets. It is believed that high fibre diets enhance gut development and gizzard function, which in turn help reduce aggressive behaviour in hens.

Egg Drop Syndrome

The only signs of egg drop syndrome appear in the eggs. Laying hens who outwardly appear healthy will begin producing eggs that either lack shells or have too-thin ones. Some hens might experience diarrhea shortly before thin-shelled eggs start appearing. According to the University of Florida extension website, researchers believe egg drop syndrome originally resulted from chickens inoculated with contaminated vaccine. Egg drop syndrome can pass from asymptomatic hens to their otherwise healthy chicks, the chicks spreading the virus in their stool. While no treatment exists for egg drop syndrome, a hen will usually resume quality egg production after she has gone through a molt.

Caged Layer Fatigue

Always feed your laying hen nutritious feed that is specially prepared for laying hens. This is not only helpful for better egg production but also help to keep your hens healthy. Many diseases affect the flock due to nutritional imbalances in homemade cheap feed. Especially laying hens suffers much due to lack of proper amount of phosphorus and calcium ratio. If you notice any hen which is alert but unable to move, then she might be suffering from caged layer fatigue.

If not treated timely, she might die by dehydration. Move the affected birds to another cage and supply her fresh water and quality feed. If you use cheap, low quality homemade feed, replace it as soon as possible and serve quality feed. This will help you avoiding further instances of diseases in your flock. Raising you flock in free range system can be helpful for preventing the disease.

Rickets

Your laying hens can be affected by rickets disease due to lack of vitamin D or proper ratio of calcium and phosphorus in their regular feed. Soft and bowed bones, thin shelled eggs, lameness, fractured limbs, low egg production etc. are symptoms of this disease. If you feed your flock commercially prepared layer feed, then chances of getting affected by rickets disease is less. Because most of this commercial layer feed contain proper ratio of all necessary nutrients, vitamins and minerals.

Egg Peritonitis

If the peritoneum or abdominal lining get infected and inflamed, then Egg peritonitis might occur in your laying hen. Usually this occurs because a yolk did not head out the oviduct of your laying hen as it should and went into the abdominal cavity. Odd stance or swollen abdomen is the symptoms of Egg Peritonitis. You can try antibiotics. It will fight with the infection and drain the abdomen. But in most cases, the laying hens die that is affected by egg peritonitis.

Coccidiosis

Coccidiosis is one of the most common and economically important diseases of chickens worldwide. It is caused by a parasitic organism that damages the host's intestinal system, causing loss of production, morbidity and death. This disease has a major economic impact on the global poultry industry.

Coccidia life-cycle

Coccidial parasites are protozoa belonging to the phylum Apicomplexa. Chicken coccidiosis is caused by seven species, all from the genus *Eimeria*: *E. acervulina, E. brunetti, E, maxima, E. mitis, E. necatrix, E. praecox* and/or *E. tenella*. The life-cycles of these species are direct. Chickens ingest sporulated oocysts (the parasite 'egg') from contaminated litter, and these pass into the intestinal tract, where the parasites invade the cells of the intestinal wall.

Several cycles of replication occur which lead to the formation of new oocysts which are shed in the faeces. Depending on environmental conditions (including temperature and humidity), the oocysts sporulate and become infective. The entire cycle takes 4 to 6 days. This short, direct, life-cycle combined with the potential for massive replication during the intracellular phase, makes this group of parasites a serious problem under intensive farming conditions.

Intestinal damage

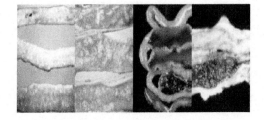

The following photos show intestinal damage caused by various species of *Eimeria* in chickens. *Source: The Merck Veterinary Manual*

E. acervulina E. brunetti   E. necatrix   E. tenella

It is the replicative phases of the parasite which lead to damage in the intestinal tissues. Individual birds may show no clinical signs, or may suffer a mild loss of appetite, weight loss or decreased weight gain, diarrhoea (which can be bloody), dehydration and death.

Resistance develops rapidly and infections can be self-limiting, but naïve birds which consume large numbers of oocysts can be severely affected and die. Immunity is strictly species-specific which means that birds exposed to one *Eimeria* remain susceptible to infection from all other species.

The degree of injury caused by the seven species varies, with some developing deep in the intestinal mucosa, causing wide-spread damage and distinct gross lesions (e.g., *E. tenella*). Other species are less destructive but may still have a significant impact on production. All species are potentially of importance economically.

The following diagrams show the intestinal sites parasitized by various species of *Eimeria* in chickens.

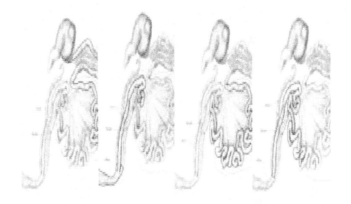

Methods of Control

Eimeria are present world-wide, and are ubiquitous under intensive farming methods. Up to six species have been shown to occur simultaneously on one farm. The omni-present nature of *Eimeria* precludes eradication as a practical option for control. Since species-specific immunity develops rapidly, the management of coccidiosis aims to achieve a balance between allowing natural immunity to build up and preventing high oocyst exposure to naïve birds. Hygiene, anticoccidial drugs and vaccines all play major roles.

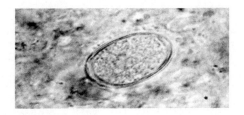

Oocysts of E. maxima Source: The Merck Veterinary Manual

Hygiene

As species of *Eimeria* have direct life-cycles, mechanical transmission is the primary means of spread between farms and between sheds on a farm.

Oocysts are resistant in the environment, both to climatic extremes and disinfectants, and can survive for weeks in soil. However, they only last for days in litter due to heat caused by fermentation and the presence of ammonia. Good hygiene, such as cleaning boots and exchanging clothes between sheds, and the eradication of rodents, assists in minimizing the transmission of oocysts. Effective farm management, such as well maintained, drip-free water lines, minimizes the level of infective oocysts in the litter, as desiccation significantly reduces sporulation.

Anti coccidial Drugs

Chemotherapy has been the main approach for controlling coccidiosis in chickens. Anti-coccidial drugs are usually used preventatively and if a farmer were to wait for overt signs of disease before treating the flock, morbidity and mortality would be high and the economic damage already done. Almost all commercial, intensively farmed flocks are administered anti-coccidial drugs prophylactically. When given at the correct low preventative doses, *Eimeria* species are able to complete their life-cycles without large numbers of infective oocysts building up in the environment. Such subclinical infections result in the development of strong, specific natural immunity without overt disease.

Vaccination

Live, virulent vaccines have been utilized since the 1960s and live attenuated vaccines have become available since the 1980s. The attenuated strains have been selected for rapid passage through the host. Consequently, they have low reproductive potential and have lost their virulence, but still have strong immunogenicity. Importantly, they cause no post-vaccinal decrease in weight gain, and are therefore suitable for use in broiler flocks.

Fatty Liver Syndrome

Fatty liver syndrome occurs through accumulating too much fat in the liver of a hen. Hemorrhaging and death are the symptoms of this disease. Hens have pale combs which is affected by fatty liver syndrome. Feeds containing too much carbohydrates can results much fat in your laying hens. Decrease the amount of carbohydrates in their feed and slightly change their feeding habit. The chickens that are raised in cage method system, affect much by this disease. On the other hand, free range chickens suffer less by this disease.

Fowl pox

Fowl pox is a relatively slow-spreading viral infection that affects most bird species, including all commercial forms of poultry. It occurs in both a wet and dry form. The wet form is characterized by plaques in the mouth and upper respiratory tract. The dry form is characterised by wart-like skin lesions that progress to thick scabs. The disease may occur in any age of bird, at any time. Mortality is usually not significant unless the respiratory involvement is severe. Fowl pox can cause depression, reduced appetite and poor growth or egg production. The course of the disease in the individual bird takes three to five weeks.

What causes fowl pox?

Fowl pox is caused by an avian DNA pox virus. There are five or six closely related viruses that primarily affect different species of birds but there is some cross-infection. Infection occurs through skin abrasions or bites, through the respiratory route and possibly through ingestion of infective scabs.

It can be transmitted by birds, mosquitoes or fomites (inanimate objects such as equipment). The virus is highly resistant in dried scabs and under certain conditions may survive for months.

Mosquitoes can harbour infectious virus for a month or more after feeding on infected birds and can subsequently infect other birds. Recovered birds do not remain carriers. A flock may be affected for several months as fowl pox spreads slowly.

Prevention and treatment of fowl pox

There is no treatment for fowl pox and prevention is through vaccination of replacement birds. Where preventative vaccination is used, all replacement chickens are vaccinated when the birds are six to ten weeks of age and one application of fowl pox vaccine results in permanent immunity.

Vaccination of broilers is not usually required unless the mosquito population is high or infections have occurred previously. Chicks may be vaccinated as young as one day of age. During outbreaks, unaffected flocks and individuals may be vaccinated to help limit the spread. If there is evidence of secondary bacterial infection, broad-spectrum antibiotics may help reduce morbidity and mortalities. As mosquitoes are known reservoirs, mosquito control procedures may be of some benefit in limiting spread in poultry confined in houses.

Lice and mites

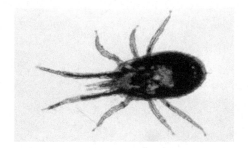

Lice and mites are common external parasites of poultry. Lice are insects, while mites belong to the same family as spiders. There are a large number of lice and mite species that can infest poultry under the appropriate conditions. They are either bloodsuckers or live on dry skin scales, feathers or scabs on the skin.

Adults can survive for 4-5 days away from the host. Therefore, infestation can be spread by direct contact between birds but also through contact with infested litter etc. They are more common and difficult to control in floor-based housing systems than in cage systems. Symptoms of infestation can include scratching, poor feather condition, unthriftiness, nervous behaviour and anaemia can occur with severe blood-sucking infestations.

Prevention and treatment of lice and mites

Flocks should be kept away from backyard or wild birds and individual birds examined regularly for adult parasites and eggs. Infestations can be treated with appropriate chemical pesticides, either as dry powders or liquid sprays. Effective bio-security procedures such as an all-in/all-out clean out between flocks will help manage these pests.

Newcastle disease

Signs of ND – conjunctivitis, depression and neurological signs

Newcastle disease is a highly contagious viral infection that affects many species of domestic and wild birds to varying degrees. The disease can result in digestive, respiratory and/or nervous clinical signs, which range from a mild, almost in apparent respiratory disease to very severe depression, drop in egg production, increased respiration, profuse diarrhea followed by collapse, or long-term nervous signs (such as twisted necks), if the birds survive. Severe forms of the disease are highly fatal.

What causes Newcastle disease?

Newcastle disease is caused by a paramyxovirus that can vary in pathogenicity from mild to highly pathogenic. Spread is usually by direct physical contact with infected or diseased birds. The virus is present in manure and is breathed out into the air. Other sources of infection are contaminated equipment, carcasses, water, food and clothing. People can easily carry the virus from one shed or farm to another. Newcastle disease virus does not affect humans in the same way that it does birds but it can cause conjunctivitis in humans.

Prevention and treatment of Newcastle disease

There is no treatment for Newcastle disease, although treatment with antibiotics to control secondary infections may assist. The virus can remain alive in manure for up to 2 months and in dead carcasses for up to 12 months, however it is easily killed by disinfectants, fumigants and direct sunlight.

Prevention relies on good quarantine and bio-security procedures and vaccination.

Newcastle disease vaccination of commercial egg layer chickens has been made compulsory.

Identifying poultry disease through poop

White Diarrhea in Chickens Causes & Cures

We are about to discuss the topic and that's white diarrhea. White poop can trigger too many things. A healthy chicken poop is firm solid in consistency and having a white cap of urates on top of it. That's normal poop. Sometimes chicken diet gives changes into colors like most often chickens who like to eat dark fruits or vegetables will poop blue, purple poop. That's nothing to worry when you are giving plenty of dark color fruits chicken poop will be dark as well. Drinking Lots of water in 100 -109°F temperature makes chickens overheated and they start releasing their heat through poop, in 40°C you may notice a poop like water that's also normal in summers.

White Poop is something out of the corner you may notice chicken that poop white coloured substance, and she's lethargy, in appetence and weak .You may also notice she's looking puffed up and losing weight. She's rattling wheezing and sneezing often. The Eyes are foamy or watery (not clear), clear white or cheesy liquid coming from the nostrils. That's the SYMPTOMS OF CRD, (CHRONIC RESPIRATORY DISEASE) that's cause by Mycoplasma gallisepticum (MG) is a bacteria- like organism that causes respiratory disease primarily in chickens.

CRD is highly contagious and spread like fire in flock if one show symptoms its necessary to treat entire flock .Most old chicken keepers know about CRD and very well at treating it .

CRD has 3 stages:-

Stage 1: The sudden appearance of wetness around the eye, sometimes referred to as one eye colds, may be due to Mycoplasma gallisepticum infection. One eye colds appear as wetness around the eye with minimal swelling of the eyelids. This type of eye condition may also be the result of stress factors such as drafts or vitamin A deficiency. When detected at this stage, the best treatment method is to apply an appropriate eye cream prescribed by a veterinarian. In most cases, this treatment will clear the eye within 2 days. When no response is seen, the disease is likely to progress to stage two or underlying diseases may be complicating the infection

Stage 2: As the infection progresses, further symptoms may include swelling of the orbital sinus ("donut" shaped swelling around the eye), pussy eye discharge, sticky eyelids and open mouth breathing. Afflicted birds and the entire flock should be treated when this stage of the disease is seen. Treatment involves the administration of a combination of antibiotics (e.g. doxycycline hydrochloride and tylosine titrate) into the drinking water for 7 days. An appropriate eye cream is applied to those birds with eye symptoms for 2 days. To accelerate recovery and help reduce the effects of any stressful factors, Turbobooster and E-powder should be mixed into a seed treat each day for 7 days.

For stage two of this disease this treatment should give a good response. A poor response indicates that underlying stress factors remain and if not seen to, the disease will progress to stage three.

Stage 3: More advanced symptoms of Mycoplasma gallisepticum infections include a swollen cere, red eyes, cheesy eye discharge, pasted eyelids and an open (gaping) mouth. These more serious symptoms are a good indication that complicated CRD is present and these birds will not respond well to treatment. Those birds with longstanding and complicated Chronic Respiratory Disease should be culled as it is too late for a full recovery and they will spread the disease to other birds in the flock.

The remainder of the flock should receive a 5 day treatment course as described for stage two of this disease. Birds that have recovered from clinical signs of the disease have some degree of immunity. Such flocks, however, carry the organism and can transmit the disease to susceptible stock by direct contact or by egg transmission to their progeny. The complicated form of CRD occurs when other underlying diseases are involved. A virus infection called Infectious bronchitis (IBV) is a highly contagious disease causing acute illness, coughing, sneezing and impaired kidney function. IBV may precipitate outbreaks of Mycoplasma gallisepticum, although when present together, mortality in adult flocks is negligible. There is however, a marked reduction in egg laying and mortality in broilers can be high especially during colder months.

E.coli infections have also been found to be a frequently complicating organism while other diseases which may complicate CRD include Mareks disease (Herpes), ILT (infectious laryngo-tracheitis) and Pox virus. Prevention is the key! It is difficult to prevent infections caused by Mycoplasma gallisepticum because the disease is transmitted by egg and any new birds must be free of the disease. Vaccinations have not proven to be a successful preventative measure because CRD is so often complicated by underlying diseases. Careful management strategies that minimise stress and the ability to determine the stage of CRD are important preventative measures in the treatment and long term prevention of Mycoplasma gallisepticum infections. The attached health programmes help to protect flocks from CRD.

Home Cures :- • Capsicum• Garlic• Turmeric powder• Oragano / Oil• Mint Tea• Fennel Tea• Black Pepper• Apple Cider Vinegar thus provided home cures will able To Prevent The Mild Cases & Give Immunity Boost In Serve Or serious infections Medication is for 3-5 days .

Medication For CRD:- • Tylan• Tylosin• Doxycycline• Oxytetracycline• NeoDox (Neomycin & Doxycycline) Best For Deep Seated Infection (Repeat After 4th Week In Chicks)• Tetracycline• Betryl.

Coccidiosis is by far the commonest cause of severe diarrhea and mortality in birds and it's mostly characterized by blood or mucous in stool. A greenish diarrhea could indicate infection with a form of Newcastle disease that affects the gut, while a whitish pasty diarrhea indicates infection with gumboro.

White or clay-like stool is caused by a lack of bile, which may indicate a serious underlying problem. Bile is a digestive fluid produced by the liver and stored in the gall bladder. Stool gets its normal brownish color from bile, which is excreted into the small intestine during the digestive process.

Gumboro diseases

Infectious bursal disease (IBD), also known as Gumboro, is a highly contagious viral infection that is found in chicken flocks in most countries. The severity of the disease will depend on the age and breed of chicken (White Leghorns are more susceptible than broilers and brown-egg layers) and the virulence of the virus. Signs of the disease can include a rapid drop in feed and water consumption, mucoid (slimy) diarrhoea with soiled vent feathers, ruffled feathers, listless chicks with unsteady gait or sitting in hunched position, picking at own vent and sleeping with beak touching the floor. Infections before 3 weeks of age are usually subclinical (no detectable symptoms).

Chickens are most susceptible to clinical disease at 3-6 weeks and severe infections have occurred in Leghorn chickens up to 18 weeks old. Early subclinical infections are the most economically important as the disease can cause severe, long-lasting suppression of the immune system. Chickens that are immune suppressed by early IBD infections do not respond well to vaccination and are more susceptible to other diseases, including those that don't normally affect healthy chickens. In clinical infections, onset of the disease is sudden after an incubation of 3-4 days.

Mortality is usually low but has been reported to be as high as 20%. Recovery from the disease usually occurs in less than a week; however broiler weight gain is delayed by 3-5 days. The presence of maternal antibody (antibody passed to the chick from the mother) will modify the way the disease progresses. The virulence of field strains varies considerably. Very virulent (vv) strains of the virus that cause high mortality and morbidity were first detected in Europe, and have not yet been detected in Australia.

What causes infectious bursal disease?

Infectious bursal disease is caused by a birnavirus (IBDV) that is most readily isolated from the bursa of Fabricius which is an organ of the immune system. The virus can also be isolated from other organs. It is shed in the faeces and spreads between birds or by contact with a contaminated environment and is possibly also carried in dust. The virus can be transferred from house to house on fomites (any inanimate object or substance that is capable of carrying infectious organisms from one individual to another) and rodents. The virus is very stable and difficult to eradicate. There is no vertical transmission (from parents directly to offspring) and mealworms and litter mites may harbour the virus for 8 weeks. Infected birds shed large amounts of virus for up to 2 weeks after infection.

Prevention and treatment of infectious bursal disease

There is no treatment for IBD but support therapies such as vitamin and electrolyte supplements and antibiotics to treat any secondary bacterial infections may reduce the impact of the disease.

Depopulation and rigorous disinfection of contaminated farms have achieved some limited success in preventing disease spread. Prevention is through good bio-security and vaccination, including passive protection via breeders and vaccination of progeny depending on virulence and age of challenge. In most countries, breeders are immunized with a live vaccine at 6-8 weeks of age and then re-vaccinated with an oil-based inactivated vaccine at 18 weeks.

Birds that have recovered from a natural infection have a strong immunity. If maternal antibody was still high at the time of vaccination, immunity in chicks that receive live vaccine can be poor. Due to the high degree of variation between naturally occurring IBD viruses there are a number of vaccines available. Vaccines need to be selected based on the types of viruses present in the area. The disease is believed not be present in New Zealand. The Australian field strains of IBD are relatively mild and live vaccination of broilers is not regarded as necessary. The main method of control relies on vaccination of parent chickens and transmission of maternal antibody to the chicks.

Solutions to Common Problems in the Management of Hens

The following are some of the problems which farmers encounter. Many of them can be avoided if the farmer is informed. These problems could lead to serious economic losses if they are not addressed promptly.

Cannibalism

This is when chicken peck and injure each other. It starts when one bird gets injured and others peck it. The victim often bleeds to death.

You can prevent this by trimming the birds' beaks. Immediately remove of the injured bird to prevent serious injuries.

Cannibalism can also be brought about by protein or amino acid deficiencies, overcrowding, insufficient feed quantities and boredom.

Egg-eating

The vice of egg eating may develop if a hen lays soft shelled eggs. This happens when there is a nutritional deficiency.

For this reason, layers' mash must have a good balance of nutrients. If a hen watches another one laying an egg, it is tempted to peck at the emerging egg and break it. Once the egg is broken, hens will immediately eat it.

You need to construct proper nests to avoid this. Individual nests should be big enough to allow only one hen at a time. If communal nests are used, they should be partially covered so as to make them dark. You can also opt to use hen cages to avoid this egg eating problem.

Broodiness

Broodiness is a natural tendency where hens try to incubate their eggs. Commercial layers do not have this characteristic because it was bred out. However, once in a while, a few hens in the flock may become broody. A broody hen is unproductive and sits in the nest, inconveniencing others. Such a hen should be isolated and kept on a rough floor until it loses broodiness.

Then, it can be returned to the laying house to resume laying eggs.

Infertility

Due to either ill health or infertility or both, some hens may fail to lay eggs.

These should be removed from the flock (culling). By 25 weeks (six months), all hens should be laying eggs. Thereafter, unproductive birds should be identified promptly and culled to avoid losses caused by feeding them.

Why Are My Chickens Laying Soft Eggs?

Chickens Laying Soft Eggs Happens More In Warm Weather. Here's an interesting egg fact for you: Warm weather brings thin shells as chickens pant. That's why you see more soft or shell-less eggs in the summer. Panting helps water evaporate cooling the chicken and causing a reduction in calcium being put into egg production.

Stress Can Cause Chickens Laying Eggs to Rush

When you're raising chickens for eggs, it's best to keep them as stress-free as possible. A soft shell, or an egg with just a membrane, can happen when a hen rushes laying; maybe she's startled by a predator or loud noises. Remember, when raising backyard chickens, it's important to learn how to protect chickens from hawks, owls, raccoons, dogs and other predators.

Check Your Chicken's Health

Even if you have the best chickens for laying eggs, soft shells can be a sign of a sick chicken. Symptoms like soft eggs can mean disease has infiltrated your flock. It's good to perform a comb-to-toe checkup on your hens to make sure the flock is healthy.

Age Can Affect Even the Best Chickens for Laying Eggs

Older hens need more calcium. A great supplement is to feed your chickens their own shells. Save the used shells, clean and microwave them for a few seconds. When they're crispy, break them up and mix them with their feed.

You can also add more calcium into your flock's diet by purchasing a commercial feed with added calcium. Overall, the occasional soft egg shell isn't a cause for concern, just something to keep in mind.

Decrease in Egg Production: Causes & Solutions

Collecting eggs from the nest boxes is one of the great joys of chicken keeping and when the yield from the nest boxes isn't what we expect, it can be disappointing, and at times, cause for concern. A drop in egg production can be one of the first signs of a problem in our flocks and just as we pay attention to our chickens' droppings to monitor their health, so too should we pay attention to the hens' daily egg count for signs of trouble. The following are the most common causes of a drop in egg production in layers flocks with solutions where possible.

Fluctuations in egg production can be caused by a myriad of physical, behavioral, environmental and emotional triggers, some requiring remedial action and others, no cause for alarm. To determine the reason for a decline in egg production, a complete flock history and physical assessment of all birds should be performed, asking questions such as:

❖ Have any new chickens been added to the flock

❖ Were new birds properly quarantined

❖ Have there been any changes in feed, housing arrangements, weather, lighting, droppings

❖ Have there been any signs of predators or sickness such as eye discharge, sneezing, lethargy, etc.

❖ After taking all factors into consideration, the cause often becomes apparent. The following are some of the causes attributable to a drop in egg production:

DECREASED LIGHTING CONDITIONS

Light triggers a hen's pituitary gland to produce eggs. Regular egg-laying requires 14 to 16 hours of light and decreased daylight hours in autumn and winter can cause egg production to decline or stop completely. Supplemental light can be added to the coop to encourage egg-laying with no detrimental effects to the hen despite commonly parroted myths to the contrary.

MOLTING

Molting is the natural process of feather shedding and re-growth. Hens divert protein and energy away from egg production to concentrate on feather growth. Supplementing a hen's diet with extra protein during a molt can aid in feather growth and egg production.

STRESS AND CHANGE

Hens are extremely sensitive to stress and typically respond to it by putting the brakes on egg-laying. They particularly dislike change, which is a major cause of stress and decline in egg-laying. Any one of the following can adversely affect egg production: changes in feed, changes in coop layout, moving to a different farm or coop, adding or losing flock members, annoyance from a well-intentioned child, a fright from a predator, irritation from internal parasites (worms, coccidia) or external parasites,(lice, mites, rodents) violent weather, barking dogs and high heat.

BROODINESS

A broody hen in the coop can affect a flock's egg production. Not only does she stop laying eggs; the mere sight of her sitting on a nest can inspire a chain reaction of hens to brood, resulting in fewer eggs overall. Broodies should be broken properly or permitted to hatch eggs in a location away from the nest boxes to ensure a prompt return to egg-laying and to preserve their health.

DISEASE, ILLNESS, PARASITES

Hens that are ill or have parasites such as worms, coccidia, mites or lice, do not perform optimally. Taken in conjunction with flock history and any other symptoms, a drop in egg production can indicate that hens are sick or suffering from a parasite infestation.

For example: if a drop in egg production follows the addition of new chickens to the flock and no other physical symptoms are noted, a communicable disease or parasite should be suspected and investigated further.

Any time a sick chicken dies suspiciously, a necropsy (post mortem exam) of the deceased bird(s) should be performed by an animal pathology lab. Always preserve the body for a necropsy by keeping it cold, never frozen, until further instruction is received.

EGG HIDING

Free-range or pasture-raised hens may fall into the unwelcome habit of laying eggs outside the coop in secluded locations.

EGG EATING

Everyone loves fresh eggs, and chickens are no exception. Hens often start eating eggs when they discover a broken egg in a nest box. Once a chicken gets the taste of this high-protein, nutritious snack, it becomes difficult to deter intentional egg breaking and eating.

AGE

After two years, a hen's production naturally declines. An aging flock will naturally produce fewer eggs after its first one and half years. Nothing can reverse this process.

PREDATOR THEFT

Various predators can be responsible for egg theft including: raccoons, rats, snakes, opossums and skunks. Coops should be secured with hardware cloth to ensure that nocturnal predators cannot gain access to the birds at night when they are most vulnerable.

NUTRITIONAL DEFICIENCY

The wrong feed, too many snacks/treats, overcrowding, mixing commercial layer feed with scratch/cracked corn/oats, etc. & being physically prevented from getting to the feeders by another flock member can all lead to nutritional deficiencies, which can result in a drop in egg production.

WATER DEPRIVATION

Access to clean, fresh, cool water at all times is imperative to the formation of eggs. Egg production will suffer if a hen's access is limited physically (frozen or too far away) restricted (prevented from reaching it by another chicken) or unpalatable (dirty/medicated/warm). The installation of a poultry nipple drinker can solve most water-related problems.

REPRODUCTIVE DYSFUNCTION

Disease or malfunctions of the oviduct such as egg-binding and internal laying can cause a drop in egg production. Seek veterinary help for a hen that has a swollen, water-balloon-like abdomen or signs of egg-looking junk are found.

Good management practices/tips for your layer chicken

- ❖   Allow for good air circulation in your poultry house for egg laying birds

- ❖   Layer needs on average 120 gm of food per day

- ❖   Distribute food troughs and water troughs evenly (one basin/50 birds)

- ❖   Provide grit at 20 weeks, you give your birds small, loose particles of stone or sand.

- ❖   Laying nests must be kept in dark places, collect eggs 3 times a day, allow a nest for every 5 layer hens

- ❖   Provide soft clean litter

- ❖   Store eggs with the small end facing down

- ❖   Add greens to the diet of your layers and whenever possible vitamins to their water

- ❖   Debeak your layer chicken at onset of egg laying

* Cull your Layers when egg production drops below 40%. To cull, simply means you start slaughtering your birds for meat.

Method and Importance of Lip Cutting/Debeaking

Cutting the lip of laying hens is very important. The main benefits are listed below.

* Lip cutting help to reduce mutual fights.

* It helps to prevent food waste.

❖   You have to cut your chick's lip at their age of 8 to 10 days.

❖   Cut the lip of growing chicken at their 8 to 12 weeks of age.

❖   Cut the lip of chicks 0.2 cm from their nose.

❖   Cut 0.45 cm in case of growing chickens.

❖   Cut the both upper and lower lips.

❖   Don't cut the both lip together. Cut one after another.

❖   Use block chick trimming machine to cut the lips.

Don't cut their lip two days after or before vaccination, after or before using some medicines like sulfur. Don't cut the lip if the hen in a strain, and during adverse weather conditions and if the hen start laying eggs.

Serve the chicken water mixed with vitamin "K" three days before cutting lips. Wash the lip cutting instrument with antiseptic. Test the edge and temperature of blade. You have to be careful, and don't damage their eyes and tongue. Choose cold weather for cutting their lips. Lip cutting process should be observed by an experienced technician. After cutting lips, serve them water in a deep pot. Provide them some extra energy enriched feed.

Common egg shell quality problems, their causes and prevention

1. White banded egg

These eggs are the result of two eggs entering and making contact with each other in the shell gland pouch. When this happens, normal calcification (egg shell formation) is interrupted and the first egg that entered the pouch will get an extra layer of calcium, seen as the white band marking. Causes for this are:

☐ Stress in the flock;

☐ Changes in lighting, for example adding artificial light in the coop to encourage laying over winter;

☐ Diseases such as infectious bronchitis.

2.   Blood on egg shell

This can be anywhere from a few spots to a smear to an alarming amount of blood.

- ❖ Causes are:
- ❖   Small blood vessels ruptured in the hen's vagina from excessive straining. This is more common in young pullets coming into lay and overweight hens;

- ❖   Cannibalism, vent pecking;

- ❖   Sudden big increase in length of daylight (when supplementing light in winter months);

- ❖   A mite/lice infestation around the vent.

☐ **Body checked egg**

These eggs' shells got cracked during the calcification process and had a layer of calcium deposited over the crack before the egg was laid. Somebody checks are covered by a thick layer of calcium, forming an noticeable ridge or band around the egg. Body checks will increase if the hens are exited or gets startled late in the afternoon/early evening, when the egg shell formation process begins. Causes of body checks are:

☐ Stress and overcrowding;

☐ The hen's age. There is a higher incidence in body checked eggs from older layers.

4. Broken and mended egg

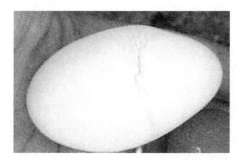

These are similar to body check eggs. The egg shell got cracked during the calcification process and mended just before being laid. Cause:

☐   Stress, frights or disturbance during the calcification process.

5.   Misshaped or odd shaped eggs

These eggs differ from the normal shape and/or size and can be either too large, too small, round instead of oval or has major changes in the shape. Shapes can range from minor, barely noticeable to grossly mis-shaped. Causes are:

☐   Immature shell gland (young layers);

☐   Defective shell glands;

☐   Disease such as infectious bronchitis;

☐   Stress, frights, or disturbances;

☐   Overcrowding in coop and/or run.

6. Calcium deposits

These egg shells have white coloured, irregularly shaped spots deposited onto the external surface of the shell. It can range from a few spots to a severe deposit, as shown in pic #6. Causes are:

☐ Defective shell glands;

☐ Disturbances and/or stress during the calcification process;

☐ Poor nutrition, for example excess calcium in the hen's diet.

7. Lack of pigment or uneven pigmentation on egg shells

The causes for this can be:

Poor nutrition: A deficiency in any of the main nutrients, protein, minerals etc in the hens' diet can influence shell colour and formation. Zinc, copper and manganese are thought to be especially important in transporting pigment onto the shell. It has been suggested that a magnesium supplement can improve shell colour:

Viral infections. Infectious bronchitis and its variants, Newcastle disease, egg drop

- Syndrome and avian influenza can cause damage to the oviduct, resulting in loss of shell colour and other problems:
- Internal and external parasites. A heavy infestation of roundworms and or capillaria worms as well as red mites, when present as a heavy infestation, can have an adverse effect on egg quality and may cause pale shells;
- Drugs. The coccidiostat drug, Nicarbazin, if present in feed, can interfere with egg shell pigmentation;
- The hen's age. And older layer will often produce eggs with paler shells, as well as a hen who had been laying intensively over a long period;
- Stress. Physical stresses, environmental stresses or nutritional stresses can all interfere with shell pigmentation;
- Exposure to sunlight and high temperatures can produce a fading effect on the shell.

8. Calcium coated egg

These eggs have an extra, powdery layer of calcium, covering either the entire egg, or just one end of the egg. Causes are:

☐   Defective shell glands;

☐   Disturbance or stress during calcification process;

☐   Poor nutrition, for example excess calcium in the hen's diet.

9. Speckled eggs

Spots or speckles can be either brown or white. They are similar to calcium deposits, except the speckles are smaller. Speckles may or may not be pigmented. Causes are:

☐   Stress or disturbance during calcification process;

☐   Poor nutrition, for example excess calcium in the hen's diet.

10.   Shell-less eggs

A shell less consists of a yolk, albumen and membrane, but has no shell at all. The egg contents are protected by the outer membrane only. These are often seen in pullets coming into lay. Causes are:

❖ Immature shell gland (young layer);

❖ Nutritional deficiency, usually lack of calcium and vitamins E, B12 and D as well as phosphorous and selenium;

❖ Certain diseases, such as Newcastle disease, infectious bronchitis, avian influenza, egg drop syndrome;

❖ Exposure to very high temperatures and extremely high or low humidity levels

An infestation of internal or external parasites, such as worms, mites or lice;

o Stress prompting the hen to lay an egg prematurely, before the shell is formed;

o Egg laying while molting;

o   Exposure to toxins, such as mold, fungi, bacteria.

11. Slab sided or flat sided egg

When two eggs enter the shell gland pouch shortly after another, normal calcification is interrupted. The second egg will not be as complete as the first and may be flattened at the side where the eggs made contact, resulting in a flat or slab side. Causes are:

☐   Disease, such as infectious bronchitis;

☐   Stress, frights and disturbances;

☐   Overcrowding in coop/run;

Sudden large increase in daily light hours, for example when supplementing light during winter months.

□ **Wrinkled eggs**

These eggs' shells have thinly creased/wrinkled surfaces. The wrinkles can range in severity from a single small wrinkle to quite a few large wrinkles, as shown in the egg pictured. Causes are:

□   Stress and disturbance during calcification process;

□   Disease such as infectious bronchitis;

□   Defective shell glands.

12.   Corrugated shell

This happens when the egg membrane is thinner than it should be, often as a result of double ovulation (two yolks) and having to stretch thinner to cover the extra egg contents. This results in insufficient plumping of the egg, leaving a corrugated membrane onto which the shell gets deposited, so the shell takes on a corrugated appearance as well. Causes are:

☐   Extra large egg size, often double or multi yolk eggs;

☐   Newcastle disease;

☐   Excessive use of antibiotics;

☐   Copper deficiency in the hen's diet;

☐   Excess calcium consumption;

☐　　　A defective shell gland;

☐　　　It is often seen with hens recovering from infectious bronchitis;

☐　　　It can be hereditary.

13.　Fart egg aka fairy egg, witch egg, rooster egg or oops eggs

These tiny eggs may or may not have a yolk. Yolk-less fart eggs are often called rooster eggs. These little eggs are often much darker than normal, as they spend more time in the shell gland pouch and gets an extra layer or two of pigment. These yolks-less eggs sometimes form when:

❖ The hen's oviduct releases a small piece of reproductive tissue or another small foreign mass enters the hen's oviduct, triggering the regular formation of an egg. The foreign object will be treated like a normal yolk and enveloped in albumen, membranes and a shell;

❖ Occasionally a hen will also lay a fart egg when something disturbs her reproductive Cycle;

❖ Young pullets may lay a fart egg or two when coming into lay and is still getting their reproductive systems in gear.

14. Soft shell eggs

These eggs are laid with an incomplete shell, sometimes just a thin layer of calcium. Causes are similar to shell fewer eggs:

❖ Immature shell gland;

❖   Nutritional deficiencies, usually lack of calcium, vitamins E, B12 and D as well as phosphorous and selenium;

❖   Disease such as infectious bronchitis, avian influenza, egg drop syndrome; an internal or external parasite infestation;

❖   Exposure to very high temperatures and/or very high or low humidity levels;

❖   Egg laid prematurely due to stress or a disturbance during the calcification process;

❖   Egg laying while molting.

14.   Mottled egg shells

In mottled egg shells parts of the egg shell are translucent, taking on a mottled or glassy appearance.

These shells can also be thin and fragile. Causes are:

☐ High humidity in the coop (make sure the coop is well ventilated;

☐ Certain diseases, (such as infectious bursal disease) and mycotoxins;

☐ Manganese deficiency in the hen's diet;

☐ Over-crowding in the coop.

16, Holes in egg shells

Pinholes, or small holes in the egg shell, may be the result of faulty laying down of the egg shell or from pimples being knocked off the shell. Possible causes are thought to be:

* ❖   Advanced layer age

* ❖   Poor nutrition

* ❖   Damage from toenails, or other sharp objects in the nest box, post laying.

Chapter 13

Accounting, record Keeping & Eggs Storage

Even if maintaining your small flock is a hobby, recordkeeping helps keep track of your expenses. It can aid in monitoring the progress of your flock. Records are important to the financial health of a business or operation. Efficient and profitable poultry operations are not guaranteed by good record keeping, but success is unlikely without them.

Records are essential tools for management to maintain a successful flock. Recordkeeping involves keeping, filing, maintaining, and categorizing inventory, financial and production information for your flock. This can be accomplished by hand recording or by using computer software.

Recordkeeping is important. Records tell an owner or manager where the business/operation has been and the direction in which it is going. Records show the strength and weaknesses of the poultry operation. They provide useful insight to financial stability for your flock. If there are any shortcomings, records will show where adjustments can be made. Along with showing where adjustments can be made and being a good reference tool, there are several other purposes of recordkeeping.

- ❖ **Purposes of Records**

- ❖ Measure profit and access the financial ability of the business/operation.

- ❖ Provides data for business/operation analysis.

- ❖ Assists in obtaining loans.

- ❖ Measure the profitability of individual operation.

- ❖ Assist in analysis of new investments.

- ❖ Production of balance sheet

- ❖ Compare performance of batches

- ❖ Compare performance for selection

- ❖ Reference to previous Successes

- ❖ Avoid previous mistakes

- ❖ Copy standard procedures

- ❖ Reference for visitors, auditors, bankers etc

- ❖ Reference to drug efficacy to certain disease outbreaks

- ❖ Compare feed efficiency

- ❖ Profitability calculation

- ❖ Shows number of birds present

- ❖ Show age of birds

- ❖ Show number of Eggs produced

❖ Mortality pattern for certain encountered outbreaks recorded for future reference

❖ Drug type and administration schedule as reference to follow for handling similar outbreaks

Records assist in avoiding management problems, helping prevent potential problems with your flock. More so, producers are being encouraged to keep accurate records about the activities on their farms due to increasing environmental concerns. Farm records consist of three distinct categories: inventory, financial, and production records. All records are used to compile useful information that is used in record analysis for an individual operation or the entire business. Records are only useful when maintained and categorized correctly.

What Should I Record?

The needs and size of your flock will determine the type of records you as an owner or manager should keep. Financial statements are an intricate part of recordkeeping. As a general rule of thumb, the larger the enterprise, the more detailed records and financial statements should be kept. Regardless of flock size, records should always be kept up-to-date. Examples of financial statements include:

1. Flock Management Plan

2. Balance Sheet

3. Farm Income Statement

4. Statement of Cash Flow

5. Poultry Enterprise Budget

Other records that should be kept along with financial records include:

- ❖ Where, when birds were acquired

- ❖ Poultry Registration Papers

- ❖ Age and number of birds in each flock

- ❖ Vaccination dates

- ❖ Vaccine expiration dates

There are several types of financial statements that can be used to help organize information for your flock. Many records are interrelated and used to create other records. In order to determine how an enterprise is doing, the balance sheet and income statement are needed.

A larger enterprise may need to elaborate by preparing cash flow statements and a statement of owner's equity. The types of financial statements used to maintain records are determined by the flock needs. Detailed record sheets may be necessary for larger flocks whereas, others may need only a basic format.

Methods of Recordkeeping

Traditionally, growers have kept records by hand. In many cases, a hand recording system is still useful for many growers. Yet, the use of computers and computer software has expanded on farms in recent years because of better record accuracy. The farm manager decides on the system that best fits his/her situation. I have listed advantages to both hand records and computer records.

Hand-Recording System

❖ low initial out-of-pocket expense

* ❖ easy to start

* ❖ requires only pencil & paper

Computer Recording System

* ❖ more accurate & faster

* ❖ much easier to create analysis

Recordkeeping can be as simple or as elaborate as you want. All farm records should provide accurate and necessary information, fit into the farm organization, and be available in a form that aids in decision-making.

Accurate records aid an owner in making good management decisions. Managing an operation requires an individual (usually the manager) to possess skills to allocate scarce resources while conducting business towards the farm.

Skills necessary for management include reducing costs of production, having knowledge of the industry, and willingness to adapt to change. Examples of scarce resources are (but not limited to) feed, water, fuel, building materials, and money. Possessing skills of a good manager allow good records to be maintained, which allow you to accomplish a specific purpose - raising and producing health birds!

DIFFERENT RECORD KEEPING FORMS USED IN POULTRY PRODUCTION

Figure 1: Management programme for layers	Apr	May	Jun	Jul	Aug	Sep	Oct	Nov	Dec	Jan	Feb	Mar	Apr	May
	18 to 20 weeks point-of-laying												Culling period	
1. Point-of-lay pullets arrive		X												
2. Give stress pack in water during arrival		X												
3. Daily inspect unhealthy chicks		X	X	X	X	X	X	X	X	X	X	X	X	X
4. Collect and record mortalities		X	X	X	X	X	X	X	X	X	X	X	X	X
5. Clean water and water bottles (always)		X	X	X	X	X	X	X	X	X	X	X	X	X
6. Ensure that enough fresh feed is available		X	X	X	X	X	X	X	X	X	X	X	X	X
7. Collect eggs	X	X	X	X	X	X	X	X	X	X	X	X	X	X
8. Record eggs	X	X	X	X	X	X	X	X	X	X	X	X	X	X
9. Order new pullets before culling or selling											X			
10. Take out the bag with manure under the cage			X	X	X	X	X	X	X	X	X	X	X	X
11. Buy enough feed a month before new flock arrives	X													
12. If needed, treat lice with Karbadust/ Blue Death powder		X	X	X	X	X	X	X	X	X	X	X	X	X

Chapter 14

Marketing Your Poultry Products

The ultimate goal of every poultry farmer is to make great sales at each harvest and unfortunately, a lot of poultry farmers get stuck at this point. They spend months raising and feeding birds; and when it's time to sell, they don't achieve much results. Not because there is a shortage of demand for their eggs or meat; but because they have not really paid attention to the sales and marketing aspects of their business.

As a poultry farmer, you should not be too caught up with the operational aspects of your business so much that you now neglect the sales aspect. If you ask me, I would say that the sales and marketing aspect is even more important after all, you are not rearing chickens for family consumption. If you are into poultry farming to earn profits, then you must pay attention to the marketing aspects of this business.

Today, I want us to discuss some of the methods that you can use as a poultry farmer to increase sales and expand your income from your poultry business. Some smart ideas include-:

1. Bypassing the middlemen

Most poultry farmers rely on middlemen to help sell their products. They sell in bulk to other people who in turn sell to the consumers. If you want to sell faster, then you should sell both in wholesale quantities and resale quantities. You can sell in retail quantities if you have your own sales outlet. Look for a good location to rent a store and then use it to stock eggs and chicken meat from your farm so that in addition to selling to wholesalers, you can also sell to retailers.

2. Take your business online

Everybody hangs around the internet these days. A large percentage of people make use of the internet around the world daily and if you want your business to thrive, you cannot close your eyes to the internet. Your social media account is a very good place to promote your business and increase awareness for your products.

I have a lady that I am following on Instagram who regularly posts pictures of attractively packaged, fresh products from her poultry farm on her page. She has a lot of followers and people keep asking her where they can get her products.

If you want to sell your products faster, you should have a strong internet presence so that people can order for products online and even those that do not order online would be able to recognize and buy your products when they see it in supermarkets or grocery stores.

Sites like Olx, facbook groups, WhatsApp groups e.t.c can be of great help in your eggs and chicken meat marketing.

3. Become a supplier to Hotels and Restaurants

Write a brilliant proposal with clearly thought-out incentives that you can offer and send it to managers of hotels and restaurants. Offer to be their major supplier of eggs and chicken meat. Hotels and restaurants always have foods with eggs or chicken on their menu and they have to get their eggs and chicken meat from somewhere.

You can help them to have access to a regular supply of fresh eggs and chicken without stress. Note that a lot of hotels and restaurants already have people supplying them, so you should think of how to outsmart these people by offering mouth-watering incentives.

4. Employ Marketers

Marketers? For a poultry farm? Yes, marketers for your poultry farm can increase your sales by more than 30%. Just employ some commission-based marketers who would earn a certain percentage from the sales they make.

5. Feed your Birds well

Yes, this is a marketing idea too. When you feed your birds well, they produce big and good quality eggs and meat which are what the consumers want. If you want your products to be top choice for consumers, then you have to pay attention to the quality of products you generate and in poultry farming; that means paying attention to the type of foods you feed your birds with because good food equals good eggs and quality meat.

6. Have your own Abattoir

Don't just stop at selling to other companies to package; nothing stops you from having your own abattoir too where you can package and brand your own products for sales and supply.

7. Advertise your products

You should also engage in advertising and promotions. You don't buy what you don't know or from people you haven't heard of. *Do you*? People mostly buy products they know or have heard about and when you advertise your products, it helps to increase awareness and subsequently, demand for your eggs and meat.

8. Carry out marketing research

Another way by which you can increase sales of your eggs and chicken meat is by carrying out marketing research regularly. When you do so, you would be able to have a clear idea of what your customer's want, areas where there is insufficient supply of eggs and things you can do to improve the quality of eggs you offer your customers.

9. Try home delivery services

Home delivery services work too. This is because a lot of people are often too busy to make trips to the grocery store and then a lot of people love their eggs and meat fresh. You can take advantage of this to offer home delivery services to people who prefer to buy fresh eggs or people who find it easier to order for stuffs from the comfort of their home. You could also serve senior citizens, the physically challenged or sick people who cannot make trips to grocery stores to buy eggs and meat.

10. Use Attractive Packaging

When designing packaging materials for your poultry products, you must ensure that it is attractive and stands out from every other product in the market. Good packaging can attract more buyers. Another thing you must know is that people look now out for nutritional information when they buy food items. So, you should consider adding some information about your products like calorie contents, protein, vitamins and all other information that health conscious people would want to know about.

How to Conduct Market Research for a Poultry Farm

Are you one of the people who are like *"But its poultry farming, why do I have to conduct a market research"?* Well, I will advice that you to drop that belief while I show you why it is very important to conduct market research for your poultry business. I would also show you how to conduct market research for your poultry farm cheaply, so that you can save some money for yourself in the process.

If you have no driving skills or experience and you are fortunate to buy a car, would you just hop into it and start driving without learning all there is to learn about the car? If you get into the car and start driving without learning and thoroughly understanding the functionality of the vehicle; *what would happen*? Well I will tell you what would happen-in some hours; you would endanger your life and wreck the car. That's not even the worse that could happen.

I just gave the illustration above for you to know how important it is to learn the ropes of any business one wants to go into and not just poultry farming alone. If you fail to do so, you would end up losing your money, your customer credibility and maybe even endangering the lives of those who patronize you.

So what does market research mean in poultry farming? This is simple. It means

Understanding *'your market'*; it involves thoroughly understanding the people you would sell to and how to reach them. It involves gathering of valuable information that would help to boost sales. People buy eggs everyday but the market is already very competitive. Therefore, you must learn the techniques to win customers over to your side especially if you are new in the business.

What Does Poultry Market Research Do for You?

1. It helps you to understand consumer behavior. You would be able to understand what they wants, who your customers are, how they make their buying decisions and how they react to changes.

2.   It would give you ideas on how to expand your poultry business. You would be able to learn ways to increase your income.

3.   Proper market research also properly positions you to beat your competitors. It helps you to "*spy*" on your competitors so that you can develop a better strategy.

4.   Market research also helps you with pricing your products. You may not be able to penetrate the market if your products are not priced properly. Highly priced products can be a turn off for consumers while products that are too low in prices would also raise suspicions of quality and become a turn off to customers too. There is the need to find a balance and you need adequate research to do this.

5.   You would also be able to discover trends and best practices in the industry to adopt so as to make your business prosper.

How to Conduct Market Research for a Poultry Farming Business

Conducting a standard market research is expensive. You would need to engage the services of experts who may charge you thousands to get the job done but there are cheap ways to conduct a market research for your poultry farming business by yourself without hiring experts. Some very cheap ways to do it includes-:

a. Research reports

You should look out for already written research reports by other people. There are a lot of websites that have such reports if you are willing to search. But if you are using a market research report written by other people, here are some important points to note-:

☐　　The reports must suit your own market. For instance, you can't use a Chinese report for a

Nigerian Market because the culture, taste and preferences of the Chinese people are different from those of Nigeria.

☐　　You must check the dates to ensure that it is a recent report. A market research done in 2018 would most likely be useless in 2020 because a lot of things would have changed.

☐　　Ensure that it is from a reputable site; preferably a government-owned institution's website so that you can be sure of authentic and genuine information.

b. Learn from others

Another way to conduct market research for your poultry farm is to learn from others who are already in the industry. You can learn a lot from the experiences of other people. Join trade unions, read industry publications, network and ask questions from other people while you use their opinions as a basis to form your own opinions.

c. Personal Research

Another cheap method is to conduct personal research. Buy some very good boots, fuel your vehicle and be prepared to move around. A camera, a voice recorder and a notbook to record your findings is also a necessity. What you would do is to visit stores where poultry products are sold and observe how buyers make their choices, *what products attract the highest buyers?*

☐ *What is unique about that product and why are people choosing it?*

☐ *How is the product priced?*

☐ *How does the packaging look?*

☐ *What is written on its label?*

When you do these for some days, you would be able to draw your conclusions and have an idea of how to package and price your products to attract buyers.

d. Personal Interviews

You can also learn a lot from potential and existing consumers by talking to them. Visit people's homes and offices and talk to them about existing poultry products *what they would rather have differently*?

☐ *What they feel about prices?*

☐ *How they would react to new products and what they feel about price increase and decrease?*

These questions when answered would help you understand consumer behavior better.

e. **The internet** is also a good place to conduct a market research for your poultry products. You can find a whole lot of information on the internet that would guide you in making informed decisions.

f. **Product testing**

This is a practical way to conduct market research. It involves producing small quantities of your products to observe how it would do in the market. If you want to produce eggs for example, you can start with few birds so that you can produce small quantities and release it to the market for sale. The way the product is received would give you an idea of how to improve the products and whether you should go commercial or halt the process.

g. Employ Consultants

Although this costs money, it is totally worth trying. It involves engaging the services of experts to carry out a market research specifically for your business.

h. Surveys and Questionnaires

You can also use surveys and put out questionnaires to further understand consumer behavior. There are websites where you can put out surveys and get results for free.

i. Social Media

A lot of people flock around social media and a lot of companies have been getting impressive results from conducting market research through social media. Websites like LinkedIn, Twitter and Face Book are very good for conducting market research.

Chapter 15

Farm Staffing and Manpower

A lot of Entrepreneurs are usually faced with fear when hiring their first employee. In fact, one of the business processes entrepreneurs dread most is the process of recruiting employees. A survey carried out recently revealed that finding good employees was one of the major business challenges entrepreneurs face when starting a business from scratch.

No matter how brilliant or promising your business enterprise might be, you cannot grow it all alone. Although you may try at first, you will soon realize that it's impossible. Every successful and famous entrepreneur built successful and flourishing companies with the aid of great employees.

It is possible for you to invent and even commercialize a business idea or concept all alone. But with time, the tasks involved in getting the business going will become much more than what you can handle single-handedly. At that point, your best bet will be to find and hire the right employees to help you achieve your business goals and entrepreneurial dream.

So, get it clear: even if you have started your business as a one man show, you will certainly reach a point when you need extra hands to help; unless you have no plans to grow your business. Finding the right employees is critical to your company's success. You need hard-working individuals with the skills, attitude, and integrity needed to boost production and sales.

Hiring the wrong person interferes with far more than just the position for which they were hired. Teams must be able to work together productively and amicably. However, it is a well established fact that job recruiting can be a time-consuming, frustrating, and expensive process when not done correctly. These tips will help make the most of your recruitment process, thereby ensuring that your business hires the best person for the job.

The above statements drive home the point that hiring the best people is now more critical than ever. If you make bad or biased hiring choices, you will lose a lot of time, money, and good results.

In fact, the cost of a single bad hire was put at anywhere between $25 to $50,000, according to a Forbes article.

The process of hiring employees is expensive. Finding, interviewing, engaging, and training new employees require huge costs. And the only way to get back what you have invested in the hiring process is to select efficient employees that will bring results. Apart from hiring costs, you will also need to get desks, computers, phones, and other related equipment for each employee. And most important are the largest costs of being an employer—salaries, taxes, and benefits. In essence, employees are a huge investment in themselves.

Since the success of your business hinges largely on the quality of employees you hire, you must be very careful during the selection process, so you can hire employees that will turn out to be assets to your business.

What is the Best Way to Hire Employees?

When it comes to hiring employees, there are three ways to go about it. They are:

☐ **The traditional hiring method**-: This involves the age-long process of running recruitment ads, screening applicants face to face, conducting exams and interviews, training chosen prospects, etc. This method is the most expensive and cumbersome of the three.

☐ **The online recruitment method**-: In this case, all the processes listed in the method above will be conducted; but they will be done online. Thus saving cost, time and resources. This method usually favors small and medium scale enterprises, online businesses or stores, work from home jobs, etc.

☐ **The outsourcing approach**-: In this case, the entire recruitment process is outsourced to a third party company, thus allowing the parent company concentrate on their core.

Each of these approaches has its pros and cons; and none can be said to be the best over the other. So it is best to choose which hiring method suits your business based on your objectives, goals, needs, capital at hand, and size of the business.

Now, what is the best way to find the right employees with the best skills, experiences, and ability to contribute to the success of your business? There may not be a one-size-fits-all answer to the question, but I recommend a strategy that I call *"the 7 C's formula"*. Here are the components of the formula:

7 Key Traits to Watch Out For When Hiring Employees

a. Competence

This is the first factor to consider in a potential employee. *Does she have the necessary skills, experience, and education to effectively play the roles expected of her*? Remember, an employee can only play her roles well when she has passed through a background that has prepared her for what the role entails.

b. Capability

Having the background required to man a job position is one thing, but having being capable of completing the tasks is another. Your ideal employee must be able to effectively handle and complete not only tasks, but also tasks that require more effort and creativity. For me, capability means the employee has the potential for growth and the willingness and ability to take on additional responsibility to take your poultry business far.

c. Commitment

A candidate can only contribute to the success of your business if she's committed to her job. And her willingness to work with you for the long term can help you determine this. If you ask what her plans for the next five years are, and she tells you that she hopes to be with a bigger company by then or she hopes to have started her own small business, then she won't be committed to your business and she won't be a good employee. You can get a clear insight into her likelihood to stay with your business for the long term by simply checking her past employment history. If she's been hopping from one job to the next, she will most likely leave you for the next available offer.

d. Character

You won't get on well with an employee whose values and character doesn't align with yours. During the hiring process, test candidates for honesty, patience, selflessness, integrity, submissiveness, and ability to play on well with a team.

e. Compatibility

Another important factor to consider when hiring new employees is their compatibility with their work environment and people that matter to the business. *Can this person get along with colleagues? Can she get along with existing and potential clients and partners? Can this person interact well with customers?* Another critical factor to consider is the person's willingness to work with you, her boss. If she can't work with you, there will be problems— even if she gets on well with other employees.

f. Compensation

During the hiring process, ensure that your chosen candidate agrees to a fair compensation package that is in line with market rates. If not, she will feel unappreciated and dissatisfied with the job, and this can lead to serious consequences, as she will not put in the best you expect from her.

g. Culture

Business has a culture or a way that its employees and management interact and behave with each other. This culture is based on the business's policies, procedures, and values that influence the behavior of a leader and employees. If a candidate shows signs that she cannot reflect your company's culture, then she would turn out difficult and disruptive.

Hiring the Best Workers for your poultry Farm –

Lessons from the Mafia Manager

At this stage, I will be share with you 16 lessons to recruiting or finding good employees; which I learned from the book "**The Mafia Manager.**" There are many business lessons in the Mafia Manager but I will specifically be extracting the lessons on hiring good workers. If you have not read the book "**The Mafia Manager**"; then you are definitely missing some uncommon business lessons.

The Mafia Manager is a book containing the distilled wisdom of men who have managed one of the largest, most profitable and long lived cartels in the history of capitalism. The Mafia Manager gathers for the first time in one book the knowledge and precepts of the ruthless bosses whose genius at organization and management contributed far more to profitability and growth than the brute strength or conventional wisdom of the legitimate CEO. If you are ready to learn, then please read on.

1.   It is not necessary to have a large family with many soldiers and button men. In fact, the fewer employees you have, the fewer betrayals or disappointments you will experience. Many employees, many betrayals, many disappointments and also higher overhead.

2.   Your staff must be of the highest possible quality in critical positions. One good man is, of course, better than a hundred fools.

3. For a truly responsible job involving others in its performance; don't hire someone just out of school or out of college, no matter how impressive his record. Hire the person who already has demonstrated an ability to work with others.

4.   For jobs less critical to the success of your organization, you will want to hire a good attitude before experience. Attitude reveals itself in a number of ways. For example, if an applicant asks about salary early on in his first interview; his is a bad attitude and moreover, he is stupid.

5.   For a truly vital job, don't hire a high powered expert; no matter how impressive his credentials. Experts care only about their credentials and their fees; and their caring never stops.

6.   Don't hire more than two members of a household (except possibly your own) and never hire lovers or husband and wife; no matter how necessary their individual skills may be to your business.

7.   Before you hire, you will interview. Knowing what skills and performance you want from the person you will hire, give applicants time to think about your questions on those matters.

8.   Be specific in your questioning. Generalities begat general (thus useless) responses.

Require applicants to be specific in their answers. Use the questions "why" and "how" to follow up responses.

9.   As for the interview strategy itself, seat applicants beside you if possible; rather than across the desk from you, in order for you to better gauge his reactions. Pick up his/her resume, frowning every now and then as if pondering on something. When this bit of play acting is finished; and the applicant suitably is unsettled by it, begin by asking the applicant why he wants the vacant job and why he feels qualified to do it. Let him sell himself as much as he wants to; interrupting only with specific questions.

Finally, if the applicant is presently working, ask him why he wants to change jobs.

10. If the applicant should frown, squirm or stroke his cheek with apparent concern while you are outlining the job difficulties; you should begin kissing him off. In polite language, let your feelings be known to the applicant. Unless the applicant tries to sell him back into contention, do kiss him off. Tell him you have others to interview and you will let him know, one way or the other in a day or two.

11. Also kiss off any applicant who is full of questions about his career's future with you.

12. In any case, close interviews when you have found out all you need to know; whether this takes five minutes or fifty.

13. When an applicant seems worth another look, check out his business references and employment history. Forget about personal references; he's not going to list someone who will bum rap him. If you happen to know one or more of his personal refs, a call or two may get you some useful inside info.

14. Bring in the most likely candidate for a second interview, preferably at lunch and at this meeting; zap him with

whatever you may have turned up bogus in his business references or employment history.

15.   If those doubts; real or imagined are resolved to your satisfaction, sell the job to the applicant. Sell the job; make no promises of future raises, promotions or broadening of responsibilities. What the applicant gets is what he gets; nobody, not even you have the crystal ball that works. Let him do the job applied for and we'll see what happens.

16.   Following your selling of the job, pose a few hypothetical problems the applicant may encounter on the job and ask him how he might go about meeting them. If the applicant passes muster; make an offer and hire him. If not, back to the office to schedule a second interview with the next most likely candidate.

And lastly, never you hire someone of the opposite sex in hopes of future erotic reward. It might be the beginning of the end for your business.

Chapter 16

Tips of making your Poultry business more profitable

Poultry farming is profitable alright, but a lot of people still fail and incur lots of losses in this business all the same. Poultry farming has been in existence for ages and while some people have smiled to the bank and expanded their businesses, a lot of investors have blamed themselves for going into the business. I always remind people that no business is easy. There is always the risk of failure in any business. Even if it is just selling candies; if you do not do it right, you cannot succeed at it.

Also, I always remind people that every business has its *'trade secrets'* and a lot of people fail in business because they do not know the trade secrets of their business. Poultry, just like any other business out there has its trade secrets which you have to know to increase your chances at success. Some of the trade secrets to expand your poultry business include the following-:

Start small

Don't start large scale poultry farming if you are inexperienced in the business. I have seen a lot of people make this mistake and it is wrong. They read about how people are making millions from poultry farming and then they go ahead to invest their live savings into the business. Some even go and obtain loans to start a business that they are inexperienced at.

For a business like poultry farming, you have to start small and then expand gradually as your business grows and demands for your products increase. You should also do a proper feasibility study before you go into the business. If there are too many competitors or if the supply for poultry products exceeds the demand in your area, then look for somewhere else to start your business or look for another business to start. There are several other lucrative businesses in the livestock farming industry that you can consider.

Have your own sales outlet

Another way to expand your poultry business is to have your own sales outlet and not rely only on supplying to retailers. You don't have to have too many sales outlets; you can start with just one. You can sell your own branded and fresh eggs to consumers.

Offer Mobile Sales and Delivery Services

Twenty-four hours in a day is just not enough for most of us because of the kind of busy lives we lead. Now, imagine having to cook, shop for groceries, tend to the kids and do all sort of other house chores and still maintain a 9-5 job. It's really not easy for a lot of working parents and this is why mobile sales and delivery services always works. A lot of people see such services as a live saving one; a service that brings you necessities without dealing with stress and traffic. With a van or two, you are ready to start offering such services within your area and that is also an expansion of your income.

Employ sales representatives

Don't think that your business is too small to employ sales reps or that poultry business is not serious enough to have sales representatives. Right here in my office, I have someone who brings me fresh eggs weekly and frozen chicken when I feel like having chicken.

She's a sales rep and earns commission for each item she sells. I have also been able to introduce her to my colleague and friends who also buy from her regularly. Now, her employer is a very smart poultry farmer because even when I buy from the grocery store, I only buy their products. Having a sales representative is a good way to increase awareness for your products and increase sales too.

Have your own Hatchery

Instead of purchasing day old chicks, it's more cost effective to have your own hatchery for hatching new chicks. You would be able to reduce the costs of hatching and also increase output compared to outsourcing the service to other people.

Produce your own feed

Another tip for growing your poultry business is to have your own feed mill for producing chicken feed. Chicken feed production is not so hard; if you can learn how to raise chickens, then you can learn how to produce chicken feed and if you are able to reduce the costs of producing feed, you would be able to increase on the overall profitability of your business.

Employ Experienced Staff

Another way to grow your poultry business is to employ people who are experienced to handle the operational aspects of the business. If you have a really large poultry farm, you can employ business consultants to suggest ways through which you can expand your poultry business.

Take Stock regularly

You should also keep an eye on the output from your farm. You should have a store where eggs are stored and have some people who would be in charge of stock keeping and counting the chickens regularly. This would help to prevent thefts.

Nutrition

Be sure to give your chickens the proper feed for best results. Young chickens should receive chick starter until they are around 6 to 8 weeks old, and then grower rations until close to laying age. Switch them over to a good quality layer feed to give them the vitamins, minerals, protein, and calories they need to lay those beautiful eggs for you.

Free ranging or pastured hens with plenty of room to roam will scratch out a lot of their nutritional requirements, but they will still need layer feed to keep them in top production. They should have access to greens e.g grass and will appreciate scraps from your table and garden.

Note:

Do not feed your laying hens very many treats or they will have too much fatty tissue in their abdomen. This will cut down significantly on the number of eggs they are able to produce, plus it isn't healthy for them. Corn and sunflower seeds are fine for providing extra calories during cold weather, but don't feed these during the hot weather.

Daylight Hours

Chickens naturally lay more eggs during the spring and summer when the days are long. Their internal clocks tell them that this is the best time to raise their young. You can trick them into laying eggs year round by setting up a light on a timer in their cages.

Starting in the late summer, have the light turn on to mimic daylight for around 14 to 15 hours each day.

Stress

Just as we are less productive when we're under stress, so are laying hens. If there are dogs and kids chasing them around the barnyard or predator attacks, things of this nature, your chickens will be living in a state of fear and won't feel the conditions are right for laying eggs.

It's also important to note that if you purchase laying hens or point of lay pullets, they will lay a few eggs after bringing them home (the ones 'in the works' before they left their previous coop) and then they will stop laying for about three weeks. So expect a dry spell with new hens. In general, keep them happy and stress free for the best egg production.

Determine the egg laying percentage

Egg laying percentage is always the best measure of egg-producing capacity and has the advantage in calculating the value of the hens. Relying only on the actual number of eggs produced may not be very valuable as it does not reflect the efficiency of the birds in producing the eggs.

Calculate the egg laying percentage by dividing the number of eggs laid by the number of layers and multiplying by 100. Obtained this figure on a daily basis and compute the average for the week or month. This will help in assessing the performance and setting targets for improvement. Averages below 70% means the feeds are going to waste. Always strive to achieve percentages above 80%.

Select Layers

Laying hens are nearly always noisy. They work and hunt for food all day, and are the first off the roost and the last to go to roost. They are nervous and very active, keeping themselves up to the greatest possible pitch.

An indication that the hen is laying is when the pelvic bones are soft and pliable, and spread sufficiently to allow three fingers to be placed between them. Experience has shown the hen is not laying at the time of examination if the pelvic bones are hard, bony and close together.

Select hens that are healthy; comb, wattles and face red; eyes bright and lustrous; neck not short, but medium to long; breast broad and long, sloping upward; back, long and broad; abdomen, wide and deeper than breast; shanks, well spread and rather long; well-spread tail.

Only mature pullets should be selected for laying. All birds that are stunted, undersized, lazy, weak or otherwise undesirable should be weeded out and sold, especially those that are inferior to other stock hatched at the same time.

Only hens that have proved their worth in the previous year should be kept over for a second or third year. They usually make good breeders and the breeding flock should be selected from them rather than from pullets. Too often the reverse practice is followed whereby hens that are in best condition are sold and inferior ones used for egg production. This is suicidal to profit and should be reversed.

Improve Laying Ability

Hens should be brought into laying as early as possible. Pullets that delay in coming to lay are naturally poor layers and soon burn out. Such fowls should not be used for breeding and the sooner they are taken out of the flock the better. In the long run such control helps in improving the flock and it is better to have some system of selection than to have none at all.

Put everything in readiness for egg production. Pullets and hens should be placed in their separate quarters early enough and special care taken to prevent overcrowding. This way the flocks get accustomed to their quarters and there is less danger of upsetting them when they begin to lay.

Manage Laying Stock

It is just as important to feed well for eggs as it is to breed well. Fowls do best when given plenty of space to forage in. At all times there should be abundant clean water available to the hens.

During cold weather increase the energy content of the feed by adding carbohydrates to the normal ration. As the weather grows colder larger quantities of energy are used to maintain the body heat. Egg production can continue without interruption even during extremely cold weather if the hens are fed well.

Plenty of shade should be provided during hot weather and the houses kept as open as possible so as to be cool and comfortable for roosting. Reduce the energy content of the feed by reducing the amount of carbohydrates in the ration. Hens that are molting should be fed well but should not get a ration too rich in protein because they are not laying. They do better when given a ration richer than usual in energy content. By proper management, many good laying hens can lay an occasional egg even while going through the molting.

Hens that have stopped laying should be culled out and managed differently from the rest of the flock. A layers ration and reduced exercise can start them laying again. Those that do not go back to laying within a reasonable time or lay for only a few weeks and then stop should be sold.

Manage pullets

Pullets can be fed more highly than hens during the early months of growth. At this time, they need abundant protein, because they are not only growing in flesh but are filling out their bones and either preparing for, or actually laying. A pullet is by no means fully mature when she starts to lay. It needs ample food to complete its development. Pullets should neither be forced to begin laying early nor to delay laying.

Handle birds gently

Hens should be protected against sudden changes. Excitement due to rough handling and fear from any cause are detrimental to the birds. Often the entrance of foreign objects, animals or visitors in the pens will cause disturbance, so these should be kept out as much as possible. When it is necessary to carry some unfamiliar object among the flock, this should be done gradually. Even the wearing of unusual attire, especially if this is of some flashy color, will disturb the fowls until they are accustomed to it.

Although birds on free range are not so likely to be disturbed, making sudden motions, calling loudly, or otherwise startling the fowls should be avoided. Enter the pens as quietly as possible and if necessary signify entrance by making some noise such as low whistling, so the hens are alerted of your approach.

Hens, especially laying hens, become attached to their quarters. They therefore should not be unnecessarily moved as this also affects the laying. Changes should be done with the least possible disturbance where it is absolutely necessary. When hens must be handled or carried, this should always be done at night and the fowls should be held gently with the hand beneath the breast.

Manage Broodiness

Broodiness is a characteristic of hens. Persistent brooders should be culled out and never used as breeders. But in otherwise normal hens, broodiness can be broken when necessary. One of the quickest ways is to confine the hens with a reserve male in a pen where there are no nests and feeding them well on a layers ration. Often the hens will begin to lay within a week or ten days. Under no condition should the hens be starved because it is not only cruel but also causes injuries to the hen.

Apply for Government Grants

Agriculture is something that the government is always interested in. And that is why it is not taxed and there are a lot of support programs for investors in the agricultural sector. Such support programs come in the form of government backed loans and grants. You should look out for such grants and apply for them.

Conclusion

My last word:

Take action **now**. Get out and find out. You cannot possibly find out everything you need to know about poultry farming through the internet. The reason is because; places, time and situations are different.

If anyone gives you every cost, expectations and details about this business online, most of that information will be incorrect because of the time and location differences.

Do you know? Even people in the same city are buying the same things at different prices.

Now, you get what I am saying. You have a work to do. Get out in a weekend and meet with different kind of people.

Start where it is easy...the poultry equipment and feeds sellers near to you.

Ask them as much questions as you can about their feeds, equipment and just any other things. They may even tell you about any poultry organization, association or regulation (which I can`t possibly know about in your environment).

One more step. Get their mobile numbers and let them know you may call them whenever you have any other questions.

What I am about to tell you is very important.... Get a mentor, someone who has started a poultry farm for at least two years. If you cannot get in your immediate environment because they may see you as a competitor, try and travel to the next town.

There are so many good people out there who will lovingly accept to guide you, but if you cannot find any, don`t mind if you have to pay someone.

This is very important because someone who has done something before is having a lot of experience and whenever you encounter any problem you give him a call.

That is how I operate. I have mentors in every important area of my life and business. I have their mobile line with me and get connected with them on the social media. Whenever I have a question or get a problem or incase I want to write an book, I simply reach out to anyone I think is having experience in that line.

With a call I get answers to my questions.

This way, you`ll grow faster.

Another advice I have for you is, don`t see your poultry farm as **just a farm.** Instead, see it as a **business.** It is not a farm. It is a business and everything a business man does to make his business succeed is what you have to do.

Be serious, diligent and hardworking (I know you might not love to hear this, yet I must tell you). Take proper account of your inflows and outflows, what goes out and what comes in, money, chicks, and equipments.

And finally, be a student of business. I need to hammer this very well because I know the kind of people I am writing for... the Africans, a continent of people who love entertainment but hate knowledge.

Believe me or you don`t, your success as a business man/woman (in any business), depends on **what you know**. I know what I am saying. I have been in this game called business for some good years. People fall out and get broke simply because they don`t` understand business.

Every business man is a business student.

Business is a profession, just like law or medicine. There are so many things you need to know about marketing, human relationship, leadership, cash flow management, negotiation, business positioning and tactics.

If you don`t know more than your competitors, you cannot make good money.

I wish you success in your quest to become a profitable farmer. Thanks for taking your time to read this guide. I am still writing more and more business guides that will nourish you in your business endeavors. Always keep in touch with me on WhatsApp **+2347051021299** to get more of my business guides.

Also WhatsApp me and give me your feedback about this book...

———✕———